Praise for Within Our Reach

"Rosalynn Carter humanly portrays the twenty-first century threshold we're standing on in the treatment of mental illness. In her conversational approach to neuroscientific breakthroughs, research supporting early intervention and prevention, and the advance of the recovery movement, she illuminates the avenues that will help mainstream care and end the mental health crisis."

—Mary Jane England, MD, president, Regis College, former president, Washington Business Group on Health

"One day, I predict that mental illnesses will be treated no differently than other physical illnesses. When that wonderful new era finally arrives, it will be in significant measure due to Rosalynn Carter. As her book *Within Our Reach* describes, she has fought to bring mental health out of a dark closet and into the light. Mrs. Carter inspired me to go public with my own chronic depression, a condition I have battled while serving as publisher of the *Los Angeles Times* and chairman/CEO of CNN. With new medications and therapies, most mental health illnesses can be treated successfully. Thank you, Rosalynn, for your lifetime of leadership."

—Tom Johnson, former chairman and CEO of CNN

"I am delighted that Mrs. Carter continues to highlight the importance of recovery and personhood as she did before our New Freedom Commission, thus giving hope and conquering discrimination."

—Daniel B. Fisher, MD, PhD, executive director, National Empowerment Center

"I have long admired former first lady Rosalynn Carter's tireless advocacy for people with mental illnesses. Her outstanding leadership in moving public policy related to mental health issues informed my own understanding of the importance of addressing these problems. *Within Our Reach* challenges us to look not only at how far we have come in our knowledge of how to treat mental illnesses, but how far we have yet to go to address the mental health crisis in our society— a crisis that touches everyone."

—Dr. David Satcher, former US surgeon general, director, Satcher Health Leadership Institute Morehouse School of Medicine

"Rosalynn Carter and her coauthors have made a major contribution to better understanding of mental health in America today. With their compelling emphasis on the importance of sound science, the elimination of old stigma, and critical progress in public policy, they give us genuine cause for hope."
—*Former senator Tom Daschle*

"Mrs. Carter and I worked together in the struggle to fulfill my father's dream of fairness and equity for mental health with other health conditions, which was finally realized with the passage of the Paul Wellstone and Pete Domenici Mental Health Parity and Addiction Equity Act in 2008. I was struck by her authenticity and sincere passion for mental health issues. *Within Our Reach* leaves us with real practical ideas for improving our mental health system."
—*David Wellstone, son of the late senator Paul Wellstone (D-MN)*

"Since Mrs. Carter began her work in mental health advocacy almost 40 years ago, we have developed a much clearer understanding of how mental illnesses impact the whole person. *Within Our Reach* looks at broader social conditions such as housing and employment and the needs of a person living with a mental illness within their community. This book is a powerful tool for our use as we work to eliminate the barriers that hinder so many from living a full life in the community."
—*Rosa Gil, founder, president, and CEO, Comunilife, Inc.*

"In *Within Our Reach*, former first lady Mrs. Rosalynn Carter reminds us with great passion and persistence of the importance of resilience, respect and recovery as we approach children and adults with mental illness. Our failure to get quality mental health treatment for children of all ages is driving more and more of them into a cradle to prison pipeline, where they slip away from us and into the adult criminal justice system. We must act now to save them. As Mrs. Carter reminds us, we have not a moment to waste."
—*Marian Wright Edelman, founder and president, Children's Defense Fund*

"Rosalynn Carter became a convert to the cause of individuals with mental illness along the campaign trail. She has been its champion ever since. The former First Lady makes clear that mental illness is no respecter of persons. It does not register as Republican or Democrat or affect any one race or gender. It affects us all—family and friends, communities and nations. But *Within Our Reach* makes clear that, as never before, there is hope and help available to all those who suffer."
—*The Honorable Gordon H. Smith*

"Mrs. Carter offers an invaluable record of several decades on the issue of mental health. The bulleted format provides easy access to specific topics, but one is drawn into each chapter as they culminate in a message of recovery being real and achievable."
—*Jeannie Ritter, first lady of Colorado*

"As a freshman mental health advocate, *Within Our Reach: Ending the Mental Health Crisis* is now my primer on the state of mental health in our country and the monumental challenges we face. It's not only a clear-eyed, compassionate, deeply informed call-to-arms from a woman who has been in the health care trenches for forty years, it's also a really good read."
—*Glenn Close, actress*

ALSO BY ROSALYNN CARTER

First Lady from Plains

*Everything to Gain: Making the Most of the Rest
of Your Life* (with Jimmy Carter)

Helping Yourself Help Others: A Book for Caregivers
(with Susan K. Golant)

Helping Someone with Mental Illness
(with Susan K. Golant)

WITHIN OUR REACH

ENDING THE MENTAL HEALTH CRISIS

ROSALYNN CARTER

WITH
SUSAN K. GOLANT AND KATHRYN E. CADE

RODALE

© 2010 by Rosalynn Carter

All rights reserved. No part of this publication may be reproduced
or transmitted in any form or by any means, electronic or mechanical,
including photocopying, recording, or any other information storage and
retrieval system, without the written permission of the publisher.

Rodale books may be purchased for business or promotional use
or for special sales. For information, please write to:
Special Markets Department, Rodale Inc.,
733 Third Avenue, New York, NY 10017.

Printed in the United States of America

Rodale Inc. makes every effort to use acid-free ♾, recycled paper ♲.

Book design by Christina Gaugler

Library of Congress Cataloging-in-Publication Data

Carter, Rosalynn.
    Within our reach : ending the mental health crisis / Rosalynn Carter ;
with Susan K. Golant and Kathryn E. Cade.
        p.   cm.
    Includes bibliographical references and index.
    ISBN-13 978–1–59486–881–8 hardcover
    ISBN-10 1–59486–881–6 hardcover
    1. Mental health services—United States.   I. Golant, Susan K.   II. Cade,
Kathryn E.   III. Title.
    [DNLM: 1. Mental Health Services—United States.   2. Health Knowledge,
Attitudes, Practice—United States.   3. Mental Disorders—United States.
4. Mentally Ill Persons—United States.   WM 30 C324w 2010]
    RA790.6.C365 2010
    362.20973—dc22 2009046852

Distributed to the trade by Macmillan

2   4   6   8   10   9   7   5   3   1   hardcover

We inspire and enable people to improve their lives and the world around them

For more of our products visit **rodalestore.com** or call 800-848-4735

*To my grandchildren and great-grandchildren
in hopes that they will grow up in a world free of stigma,
where all are able to get the help they need.*

CONTENTS

ACKNOWLEDGMENTS

I HAVE WORKED IN the mental health field for more than thirty-five years, and this is an exciting yet frustrating time. Over the past couple of decades, we have learned much about the brain and about the power of individuals to recover from serious mental illnesses. We have excellent knowledge about effective treatments and sound models for delivering them. Today the overwhelming majority of people with these disorders can lead normal lives in their own communities . . . going to school, working, raising families. And yet, mainly because of stigma, the respect we should show for people who have these illnesses is lacking, services are not available, and they suffer from discrimination in many areas of life. I hope this book will dispel the myths and misconceptions that keep people from treatment and hinder all our efforts to help them.

Within Our Reach is a serious book, describing what we now know and what can be done to transform the current system, which is today "in shambles." The book has been a collaborative effort, drawing on the valuable information and advice of leading authorities in the field and working with the Mental Health Program staff at The Carter Center. I rely on their knowledge and hard work to ensure the material is as accurate and up-to-date as we can make it. Invaluable input came from Thom Bornemann, Lei Ellingson, Lynne Randolph, Jane Bigham, John Bartlett, Yolonda Johnson, and especially Rebecca Palpant, who took on the added responsibility for coordinating the staff input. Alexandra Trimble, Kristen McLean, and Harden Wisebram, among other interns, were particularly helpful.

I am grateful for the help of Susan Golant, with whom I have collaborated on other books and who once again was a valuable partner in writing the book. I am especially indebted to Kathy Cade, my projects director in the White House, who has continued to be involved with me in my mental health work since we left Washington. She is familiar with the issues and was a major help with the writing. I also want to thank Shannon Welch, our editor, whose guidance helped shape the final product with the focus and clarity these complex issues deserve; Nancy N. Bailey, senior project editor, for her attention to detail; and our publisher, Rodale. Lynn Nesbit, my longtime agent, deserves thanks as well.

And last, but not least, I want to thank my husband, Jimmy, who has always approved and supported my efforts and who was very patient over the long period of time it took me to finish the book.

During my many years as a mental health advocate, I have

been privileged to meet thousands of individuals who have shared my passion for the cause. Many have struggled with mental illnesses themselves. Some have been at the forefront of expanding our knowledge base; others have developed effective new programs for care; still others have shaped more humane public policies. In writing this book and over the years, I have benefited from their words and wisdom. I take this occasion to say to my many friends and colleagues that I am deeply grateful for the opportunity to have waged this most important fight with you—to bring us closer to the goal of recovery for all. Hopefully, this book will help advance our cause.

Rosalynn Carter

This book evolved from a simple revision of our previous work, *Helping Someone with Mental Illness*. None of us realized when we decided to strike out into new territory that we would create a book of this scope and import. I am deeply grateful to former First Lady Rosalynn Carter for inviting me to work with her once again. It is such an honor to be in her presence and to witness her compassion for people who have struggled with mental illnesses—a cause she has championed for decades. I am also most grateful to Kathy Cade who worked with Mrs. Carter in the White House and who has remained her steadfast colleague. Kathy's depth of knowledge, passion, and steady voice helped shape our work throughout. I value her friendship. We are grateful to all of the experts who were interviewed and especially Dr. Tom Insel, director of the National Institute of Mental Health, who provided the spark from which this book took shape. I am also indebted to my agent, Richard Pine, at InkWell Management, who always looks after my interests. And finally I wish to thank my dear husband, Dr. Mitch Golant, whose enduring love and support provide the wellspring from which all good things emerge.

Susan K. Golant, MA

It has been an honor and a privilege to participate in the writing of this book. I am humbled by the generosity of all those who provided wise counsel, advice, and support to me, and I am deeply indebted to each of you. Susan Golant has been a gracious partner, sharing her literary expertise throughout, and I am grateful to her. Mrs. Carter gave me a lovely gift— the chance to once again work closely with her on a special project. Her dedication, her compassion, and her commitment to helping others inspires me every day. All who care about or are touched by mental health issues are fortunate to have her as our champion.

Kathryn E. Cade

A CALL TO ACTION

WHEN I BEGAN CAMPAIGNING for my husband for political office, I had no idea of the impact it would have on my life. I made enduring friendships; I learned more about our country than any civics class could ever teach me; I developed a pretty tough skin from warding off the criticisms that always come with political life; and I became interested in people and issues that I had never seriously considered.

Campaigning is not easy. It is an emotional experience, with good days and bad. The good days can sour in an instant, like the time I was standing at a factory gate very early in the morning waiting to hand out Jimmy Carter brochures to those coming to work. The first man to whom I handed a brochure flung it to the ground and shouted, "Lady, we make the B-1 bomber here." Shocked, I learned that Jimmy had announced the day before that he was against the B-1 bomber.

There were also moments of levity. One day, traveling with a friend, we saw a huge crowd of farmers gathered at a barn. We were trying to reach as many voters as possible, and we couldn't resist stopping. We made our way into the barn; they stopped in the middle of auctioning a cow and handed me the microphone. We were a big hit that day.

When you're campaigning, people pour out their hearts to you about their hopes and dreams, and especially about their problems. At first I was surprised that strangers wanted to confide in me. But I soon came to understand that I might be the only person they would ever meet who was close to someone who might be able to help them.

When Jimmy ran for governor of Georgia in 1966, many people who were in desperate need asked me what my husband would do, if elected, to help their son or daughter, parent, or other family member who was in Central State Hospital, the big psychiatric facility in Milledgeville, Georgia.

Some years earlier there had been an exposé of the terrible conditions there. Our local newspapers had been full of horror stories about the thousands of patients packed into the facility, often for a lifetime, with almost no services and only forty-eight doctors to care for them. The staff struggled to feed everyone and worked just to keep them alive; there was no time for treatment. Doctors reportedly used patients as guinea pigs, giving them experimental, unapproved drugs without their consent or the knowledge of their families. I was most distressed that children were being thrown in among the seriously ill adult patients. There were no other facilities for them. They were sent to this hospital or out of state. Otherwise, they received no treatment whatsoever.

This was a time when most people with serious mental illnesses in our country were housed in these enormous and inhumane "mental institutions." Following the exposés in our state and many others, Congress in 1963 passed the Community Mental Health Centers Act, which called for "deinstitutionalization"—closing the large, isolated state hospitals and building community mental health centers instead.[1] This sounded like a very good thing. People would be able to find help close to home.

But I discovered that people were being moved out of institutions all across the country before there were any services established in their communities. My own state of Georgia had plans to build a series of regional hospitals, but even the most basic services were available in few of our cities and towns.

Now, as I campaigned, I was approached almost daily by family members distressed about loved ones at our Central State Hospital. Over and over the questions came about what my husband would do to address their terrible problems. One day I asked Jimmy if he was getting the same questions, and he was. He said I should just reassure people that he would help them when he was elected. I did that for a while. But as the days passed, I became more and more concerned and began spending more time listening to the individual stories. Then one day, an incident set me on a course that would become a lifelong crusade for me.

At 4:30 in the morning, I stood at the entrance to a cotton mill in Atlanta, waiting for people to get off work. I saw an older woman emerge, all alone. She was small, a little stooped, and weary from work, and her clothes and hair were covered with lint. "Good morning," I said as she approached me. "I hope you're going home to get some sleep."

"I hope I can get some, too," she said. She told me she had a daughter who was mentally ill and that she and her husband struggled to make ends meet in order to care for her. "I work at night while he stays with her, and he works during the day when I'm at home," she said.

She was already exhausted after the long night, probably on an assembly line where she had to be alert at every moment. And what would she find when she got home? Would her daughter be awake? Would she be able to get any rest? I watched as she walked away.

The image of the woman haunted me all day. I kept thinking about how much she and her family suffered, and how terrible it must be for them to know that there was no end in sight. I knew it was useless for her to try to get help. There was none available. I thought about how many others must be caring for loved ones at home without adequate help. I'd been worrying about those in institutions and their families, but how many others were struggling to care for a loved one, without access to any professional services at all? The scope of the problem simply overwhelmed me.

Later in the day, while campaigning in a small town in South Georgia, I learned that Jimmy was going to be in the same town that night for a big rally. I stayed, and when his speech was over I got in line with people to shake his hand. You can imagine his surprise when he reached out his hand and saw me. "What are you doing here?" he asked.

He had to continue working his way down the long line, so I only had time to say, "I came to see what you are going to do to help people with mental illnesses when you are governor."

To this he replied, "We're going to have the best program in the country, and I'm going to put you in charge of it."

Jimmy had been touched by those he had met on the campaign trail, too, and he kept his promise. A few weeks after he became governor, he created the Governor's Commission to Improve Services for Mentally and Emotionally Handicapped Georgians. He didn't put me in charge, of course, because I didn't know much about the subject then, but I worked closely with mental health professionals, volunteers, and family members to learn about the issues. I attended all the meetings of the commission, volunteered at the new Georgia Regional Hospital in Atlanta, and visited other hospitals, reporting back to the commission members on what I found. I spoke out about the issue, trying to make it an acceptable subject of conversation.

When I first got involved, there was little understanding of the causes of mental illnesses, the complex relationship between brain development and environmental factors, or how to determine the most effective treatment. The world has changed in many ways since then. Now, functional brain scans are able to track some disorders in real time; human genomic research is charting genetic markers for mental illnesses; new insights are being forged into the powerful interactions between basic biology and the environment; and personalized medications hold promise for individuals who might have been deemed hopeless just two decades ago. We are much closer to finding causes and cures, and there is even hope for prevention. Most importantly, today we talk about recovery and recognize that most people with mental illnesses can be diagnosed and treated and go on to live full and productive lives.

Yet, despite the great medical and psychosocial breakthroughs, in some ways we have hardly moved forward since my early days as an advocate. When Jimmy was elected president, one of his first official acts was to create a presidential commission to study the mental health crisis in our country. I served as the honorary chairperson. In 1979, I went before a Senate committee to present the findings of our President's Commission on Mental Health. Meeting the needs of people with serious mental illnesses was not a legislative priority for the Congress then. The key subcommittee was chaired by the late Senator Ted Kennedy of Massachusetts, who at the time was challenging my husband for the Democratic nomination in the 1980 election. Jimmy's political advisors argued strongly that I should not appear before his committee. They worried that politics might prevail, that I might be embarrassed, that the press might focus only on the political rivalry.

I would not be dissuaded. I had to convince the senators of the tragic circumstances people with mental illnesses faced in our country and to impress upon them the great need for new legislation. I explained to the committee members the terrible situation we had found: So many people were suffering because of our failure to do anything to help them. I concluded by saying, "We have endured years of neglect of those with mental illnesses—and no other problem facing society touches so many families or leaves them so vulnerable." It was time to bring an end to this horrible neglect, and I asked for their help in passing legislation to reform mental health care in our country.

The room was filled with members of the press. The story of a First Lady appearing before a fierce political rival to promote a cause that crossed all political and party boundaries was a powerful one, and together we were able to put mental health on the front pages of newspapers and on the nightly network news.

For another full year we worked tirelessly to move legislation through Congress. Ultimately, we were successful in getting a bill enacted that incorporated many of the recommendations we made. On October 7, 1980, Jimmy signed the Mental Health Systems Act into law—the first major reform of publicly funded mental health programs since the Community Mental Health Centers Act of 1963. There is no way to describe the joy, satisfaction, and thankfulness I felt for the many people who had worked so long and so hard to make this day possible.

Unfortunately, most of the changes and improvements we had anticipated were never realized. Very soon after the act was passed, we left Washington, and within a month of inauguration, President Ronald Reagan abandoned our legislation. All that we had accomplished was lost. I was devastated. Our bill was not perfect, but it could have made a significant difference.

What are the consequences of our country's inaction? Twenty-five years later, in 2002, another presidential assessment, the President's New Freedom Commission on Mental Health, reported that the mental health system in the United States is "in shambles." When we looked at their recommendations, it was shocking to see how many of them were the same as those we had made in 1978: Filling the gaps in care for children and for elderly citizens; correcting the shortage of trained mental health professionals, especially those serving minority populations; and providing adequate support services for those suffering from serious and persistent mental illnesses, among others. The report also confirmed that stigma remained a major obstacle to progress in our field.

We have been given many gifts as a nation; we are rich beyond measure. We Americans think of ourselves as decent, generous, and compassionate people, and for the most part we are; yet we treat a large proportion of our own population as though they are second-class citizens undeserving of our help, our resources, and our understanding.

In any given year, approximately one out of every four adults in our country struggles with a mental illness, yet people with these illnesses are a hidden minority who suffer from pervasive discrimination. More often than not, their suffering and that of their families and loved ones goes unnoticed and unheeded, and that hurts all of us. Among children, fewer than one third of those who need help actually get it.[2]

In my Senate testimony in 1979, I said, "The mental health problems facing our country are the problems of all citizens. The people with these problems are ourselves, our families, our neighbors, and our friends." It is still the same. Mental illnesses do not discriminate, they touch every quarter of our society: parents, teenagers, siblings; people living in rural settings, in cities, and on Indian reservations. They touch lawyers, the clergy, and CEOs. Because this issue affects every family in America, we are all compelled to care about it and to be appalled by the lack of action and progress.

How can we leave people who are suffering from mental illness stranded without help or hope when both are within our reach? What does it say about us as a people and a nation when we don't take care of the most vulnerable among us? Why is it that we continue to discriminate against them, denying them good insurance coverage and access to care? Why are so many afraid to seek treatment or, when they do, unwilling to reveal this fact? And why is it that we keep our own struggles hidden and do not get help? Why don't we ensure that others have the services they need when we would act much differently if someone were facing cancer or diabetes or stroke?

I blame much of it on the stigma that is still associated with mental illnesses. We have all seen the pain and suffering that these illnesses can cause, yet there are so many myths and misconceptions that it's hard to get an accurate picture of them and to understand that so much has changed over the last ten or fifteen years.

Fighting to bring mental illnesses out in the open, to make available the financial and other resources needed to treat or even prevent them, to give them the same attention as physical illnesses—this has been my priority since leaving the White House. At The Carter Center I established my Mental Health Program, which has provided leadership in tackling pressing problems, such as the debilitating impact of exposure to trauma. Our annual symposia focus on major policy issues; the most recent addressed health care reform. We also have a journalism program that has brought more than a hundred talented writers, reporters, and producers together to promote more accurate coverage of mental health issues in all media— a key to finally reducing stigma. I personally have lobbied leaders in industry, Congress, and several different administrations to pass laws that will provide the same insurance coverage for mental illnesses as for physical illnesses.

Based on my years of involvement and advocacy, I know that a revolution is occurring—recovery is a real possibility for most people with mental illnesses. It is no longer acceptable for them to be marginalized. We have learned so much— about the biological roots of major mental disorders and how to provide essential services to support recovery in our communities, as well as more effective psychotherapies. We must get on with helping those who are affected and make up for the decades of neglect, inattention, and discrimination they have endured. Until we harness our energies and change how mental illnesses are dealt with in this country, until we let go of our old-fashioned ways of thinking, unless we change the conversation entirely, I fear the exciting advances that have been made over the last decade and a half will have no impact and we will lose the chance to improve the course of millions of lives.

We cannot let this happen. Ultimately, the way we treat people with mental illnesses in our society is a moral issue. To neglect those who through no fault of their own are in need runs counter to our core principles—the values of decency and equality that we hold dear. Today, with our knowledge and expertise, we have a great opportunity to change things forever for *all* people with mental illnesses by moving forward into a new era of understanding, care, and acceptance. Think of what that would mean: a real future for them, with so much pain and suffering gone, with the chance at last to live full and productive lives, free from the stigma that today still all too often tarnishes their every move.

I was fortunate to get to know the great anthropologist Margaret Mead. When she heard I was interested in mental health, she came to visit me at the Governor's Mansion and again in the White House. She said to me, "If we select for our first consideration the most vulnerable among us—the emotionally disturbed child, the person institutionalized with psychosis, the street addict—then our whole culture is humanized." She believed that our value as individuals, our success as a society, could be measured by the compassion we show for the most vulnerable among us.

Can we live up to Margaret Mead's standards? We can. Our dream of the day when stigma no longer exists, when services are available to all, and when every individual can look forward to a happy and fulfilling future is within our reach.

1.

STIGMA, PREJUDICE, AND DISCRIMINATION

Stigma: Our Biggest Challenge

STIGMA IS THE MOST damaging factor in the life of anyone who has a mental illness. It humiliates and embarrasses; it is painful; it generates stereotypes, fear, and rejection; it leads to terrible discrimination. Perhaps the greatest tragedy is that stigma keeps people from seeking help for fear of being labeled "mentally ill."

When I first began working in the mental health field in Georgia, there was such stigma attached to mental illness that no one wanted to be identified with the issue. No one wanted to talk about it, nor would anyone admit to having a family member with an illness. It was hard to get anyone involved,

1

particularly anyone with influence. So when I announced that I would be working on the issue, the advocates in Atlanta descended on me—all five of them. "We need you," they said. At the same time, they warned me that it would not be easy, and they were right. It didn't take long for me to learn just how powerful stigma is. I thought the most important thing I could do back then was to talk about the issue publicly to try to bring it "out of the closet"—make it an acceptable subject of conversation. I still believe that to be the case.

In January 1977, only a few days after Jimmy took office as president, a letter arrived for me at the White House. It is just one example of the countless letters I continue to receive and that constantly remind me of the tragic effects of stigma and of the obligation I have assumed to try to do something about it. The letter was from a woman whose brother, a twenty-six-year-old former US Marine, had recently walked out of our big Central State Hospital and drowned himself in a river adjacent to the facility. She wrote:

> The most neglected and unheard Americans are not the blacks, the women, or the poor, but the mentally disturbed. Why? Because no one listens. Is it because of their illness? Sure, they are ill, but would you discount everything a person with cancer said? I think not. But you justify not listening to the mentally ill by saying what they say is probably irrational. How do you know whether it is or not? Have you listened and checked out their story?

Having loved a person who was mentally ill, I shared the hell he lived in—the same hell others have to endure to this very day. . . . Society has compassion for the patient with cancer. The public is even being educated to have compassion for the alcoholic. This is fine, but when will our society be educated enough to have compassion rather than contempt for the mentally ill? It is as if these people are being punished for being sick.[1]

Upon rereading the letter now, I am reminded of something the late George Gerbner, PhD, who was dean of the University of Pennsylvania's Annenberg School of Communication, said at our very first conference on stigma at The Carter Center in 1985. For more than thirty years he studied television content and how it shapes perceptions in our society. He found that people with mental illnesses are depicted in an overwhelmingly negative light, which in turn perpetuates myths and misinformation that lead to the denial of full and equal rights, opportunities, and power. "That describes a human rights problem," Dr. Gerbner said, "and this is where the problem of people with mental illnesses joins one of the most critical problems of our society: . . . how to progress toward a sense of fairness, dignity, and more equitable distribution of resources to all people."[2]

Stigma runs through every aspect of mental illness: It curtails attention from elected officials and funding for programs, it underlies the persistence of myths and misconceptions about the illnesses and the people who live with them, and it is a root cause of all the inequities that remain in relation to mental illnesses.

What Is Stigma?

Otto Wahl, PhD, a longtime advisor to my Carter Center journalism program and professor of psychology at the University of Hartford in Connecticut, defines stigma as "a mark or label imposed by others that leads to devaluation and discrimination."[3] This brief definition encompasses all of the negative feelings that stigma imposes on those with illnesses, their families, and even professionals working in the field.

Otto's definition is simple and elegant, but trying to measure the impact of stigma and the many ways it harms people is much more difficult. One of the most insidious effects is that stigma gives rise to stereotypes: People experiencing mental illnesses are considered to be lacking in judgment or weak willed; they are seen as incompetent, unreliable, and unable to make decisions for themselves. It is thought that they can't work, hold public office, or even live on their own; they are dangerous, unpredictable, and violent; they have brought these problems on themselves; and they will never get better.

The truth is very different. Most people with serious mental illnesses recover and do well in the world—go to school, flourish in their jobs, own homes—yet they are considered to be rare exceptions. The stereotypic beliefs held by the general public and by many people who experience the illnesses do not reflect what modern science and other people living with mental illnesses themselves have to tell us.

Stereotypes Lead to Prejudice and Discrimination

A recent national study on stigma found that while the vast majority of Americans say they are willing to make friends with people with mental health problems, "it is equally clear that this tolerance does not extend to a willingness to accept these persons as family members or coworkers." On average, almost 70 percent of the people interviewed were unwilling to have individuals with a mental disorder marry a family member and almost 60 percent were unwilling to work closely with them.[4] These findings hardly make sense given the reality that one person in four has a mental or emotional problem.[5]

Discrimination assumes many forms. Larry Fricks, a long-time friend who lives with bipolar disease, has been in recovery for years. In Richard M. Cohen's book *Strong at the Broken Places,* which documents the lives of five people coping with devastating chronic illnesses, Larry described his dehumanizing ordeal as the object of coercive treatment during a psychotic episode.[6] "'They forced drugs on me. The doctors can do whatever they want, because the patient is cornered. . . . I was in what they called seclusion. . . . People could look at me through a small opening in the door.'" Isolated, he was kept in restraints, bound to his bed. "Being taken away in a police car, put in seclusion and restraints—these were not experiences that raised my self-esteem," Larry explained at our symposium on stigma. "The negative self-talk was so powerful, I had suicidal thoughts."

Larry also shared that he had experienced a more subtle discrimination during a meeting with a physician. "The cardiologist started talking to my wife when he discovered I was in recovery from bipolar disorder. My wife had to say to the doctor, 'Larry is right here. He can answer this question better than I can.'"

Larry continued, "What people believe about mental illness may be more disabling than the illness itself. At the core of stigma is the belief that our thought process is broken. If that's so, can you ever really trust us? Would you ever believe that I'm capable of thinking intelligently and logically about things even if I was tied down twenty years ago and psychotic?" He asked the assembled experts hypothetically, "Will you ever get over that?"

Where Does Stigma Come From?

Many of us may be puzzled about the origins of stigma and believe that we are enlightened, that we are not prejudiced against people with mental illnesses and don't discriminate. We may think it must be someone else—someone less educated, someone less tolerant—who perpetuates the problem. Yet too often, as soon as the press sensationalizes a violent episode involving someone with a mental illness, we begin to question whether "those people" are a menace to society.

Where does stigma come from? Deep down, many of us who are not affected by a mental illness are afraid of people who are. They are, on some level, different from us, and therefore we lack compassion for them. We don't want community mental health centers opening in our neighborhoods. We look the other way or cross the street when we see a disheveled homeless person sleeping on the sidewalk or talking incoherently.

I used to believe that stigma grew from ignorance and our innate mistrust of odd behavior, and I still believe these are major factors, but I have come more and more to believe that fear often underlies our attitudes and behaviors. What do we fear most? That people with psychiatric disorders will suddenly turn violent.

When it comes to violence among people with mental illnesses, we need to turn our stereotypes on their heads. People with severe mental illnesses are much more likely to become the victims of violence—assault, rape, robbery, and murder—than the perpetrators. The annual incidence of violent crimes against people with serious mental illnesses is more than four times higher than in the general population.[7]

Looking at these numbers, we have to ask ourselves, who are the victims and who are the perpetrators? Our perceptions simply have been wrong. To put this all in perspective, the overall contribution of mental disorders to the total level of violence in society is exceptionally small.[8]

Other studies confirm these conclusions. Mental illness alone does not predict future violent behavior; gender and age are greater predictors. It is estimated that only 2 percent of all the violent episodes in the United States can be attributed to people with a mental illness.[9] So why are so many of us so afraid?

The Media and Mental Illness

Where do these distortions come from? Why is it that, despite the fact that mental health problems are so common and that each of us surely knows someone who has sought treatment, there is still such fear? Part of the answer lies in the notion of meaningful contact: the frequency and nature of interactions. While positive personal experiences can help challenge and change attitudes, the barrage of negative messages coming from the mass media constantly overwhelms the benefits of these encounters. Television, movies, newspapers, magazines, the Internet—all remain primary sources of misinformation about people with mental illnesses. They distort reality and perpetuate negative stereotypes.

In 1999, Mental Health America, a nonprofit mental health advocacy group, reported on a survey performed for the Screen Actors Guild, which found that characters with mental illnesses in prime-time television shows are depicted as the most dangerous of all demographic groups: 60 percent were involved in crimes or violence.[10] Although Otto Wahl's more recent research suggests these kinds of stories are less prevalent these days, at least a third of them continue to focus on dangerousness. Also, the vast majority of the remaining shows on mental illness highlight either other negative characteristics, such as unpredictability and unsociability, or medical treatments. Otto tells us that positive stories emphasizing the recovery of people with even the most serious mental illnesses are notably absent.[11] Other researchers have found that characters with mental illnesses on TV were ten times more violent than other TV characters and ten to twenty times more violent than *real* people with mental illnesses in the United States.[12]

The impact of these findings was brought home to me so powerfully one night when Jimmy and I watched an episode of *Law and Order* that portrayed a young man with a mental illness who kidnapped a little girl and locked her in a room in an old warehouse. She wasn't killed because she was found, but the implication of violence was there. We switched to *Without a Trace,* only to find a story line that revolved around a mentally ill older man who had killed two women. Two programs at the same time were depicting situations that we know are quite rare. It was very discouraging after all the efforts we and so many others have made to educate those in the entertainment business.

Though today we are beginning to see more accurate, humane, and compassionate images in movies such as *As Good As It Gets* (1997), *A Beautiful Mind* (2001), and *Lars and the Real Girl* (2007) and in TV series like *Monk* and *The Sopranos,* we still have a long way to go before we break free of the dangerous stereotypes associated with mental illnesses.

Print media also perpetuate stigma, reinforcing on almost

a daily basis the most negative aspects of these illnesses. Otto Wahl and his team analyzed 300 newspaper articles that contained the term "mental illness." Over ten years of publications, he and his team found that coverage of stigma improved, the theme of dangerousness decreased, and articles with a negative tone became less prevalent. This seems like progress until you take into account that dangerousness remained the most common theme and that negative articles were twice as likely to be published as positive ones.[13]

In a recent study that analyzed seventy large US newspapers, Patrick Corrigan, PsyD, professor of psychology at the Illinois Institute of Technology, and his colleagues found that more stories were related to dangerousness than to any other theme. Even more discouraging was their finding that stories related to violent crimes and other manifestations of danger often ended up in the front sections of the newspapers, making them more visible to readers.[14]

At The Carter Center we have been working for more than a decade to develop a cadre of journalists who can have a significant impact on the public's understanding of mental illnesses. Our Journalism Fellowship Program encourages recipients to pursue in-depth stories and to share their knowledge with other journalists throughout their careers. Their projects have garnered numerous awards. They are bringing their expertise to media outlets ranging from the national network news to major weekly magazines, daily newspapers, radio, and even the Internet. I know that they are making important contributions in lifting some of the stigma.

The End of Stigma

Thirty years after I received the letter from the Marine's sister about his needless and tragic death, the following e-mail came to my attention. It was from Kelly Lehman, a woman in her thirties, who is struggling for dignity and fighting for recovery. She, too, attributes many of her troubles to stigma:

> If you could only witness with your own eyes the hurt, the loss, and those who have simply given up, you'd understand my urgency to STOP the stigma. Over my twenty years, I have been hospitalized many times due to my disability becoming unmanageable and every time I have witnessed the same events . . . patients in their 20s still full of life and dreams and confident in their recovery . . . patients in their 30s fighting to hold onto their dreams and terrified of their outcomes, but still fighting . . . finally patients in their 40s with no dreams left, just sadness. They have given up because no one cared, no one listens and no one fights to STOP the stigma for them.[15]

How do we stop the devastating impact of stigma? First, we need a reality check. Consider some of the very well-known and successful individuals who have had mental illnesses. Abraham Lincoln and Winston Churchill both suffered from severe depression. Churchill called his disorder the "black dog," yet both of them led their nations admirably in times of terrible war and turmoil. Kjell Magne Bondevik served as prime minister of Norway from 1997 to 2000 and again from 2001 to 2005. As prime minister, he took sick leave for a mental illness when he suffered a depressive episode in 1998. He then was re-elected and continued to lead his party—an amazing victory over the persistent obstacles of stigma and discrimination.

Florida's former senator Lawton Chiles was elected governor of that state despite disclosing that he had long been taking Prozac. He won the Democratic primary in 1990 with 69 percent of the vote and then ousted the Republican incumbent to become an active, hands-on governor. "I wish I'd known about Prozac [earlier]," Chiles said publicly, "because it helped me a lot."[16] After Alma Powell, wife of former secretary of state Colin Powell, revealed her history of depression, General Powell commented, "'It is not a family secret. It is very easily controlled with proper medication, just as my blood pressure is.'"[17] These people, though famous, are not exceptions. Every day, people recover from mental illnesses and lead productive lives.

Researchers have shown that having contact with people who have mental illnesses helps to reduce stigma because it fosters empathy. Larry Fricks relies on the model of race relations in the South to explain how this works. "When people worked next to each other and interacted with one another, it broke down old beliefs and barriers," he said. The best way to overcome stigma is to learn that the man who sits in the next office suffers from depression or the neighbor you chat with on summer evenings is battling bipolar disorder. You know them; you're not afraid of them.

Over the last fifteen years, we have studied how public attitudes about mental illness are changing. Today we have a much better understanding about the causes of these illnesses and, perhaps in part because of the work of so many advocates and organizations to fight stigma, more people are confident that they can be treated. But the sad truth is, our research shows we are not making any meaningful progress in accepting those with mental illnesses. We can only hope for this to change when more and more individuals are willing to talk openly about their experiences.

We gain understanding and compassion when a family member or a friend does this. It is also helpful when powerful people "come out of the closet" and let others know about their illnesses. Tom Johnson, the former CEO of CNN, suffered from severe depression. He described to us how he would close the door to his office and curl up in a fetal position when his condition worsened. The late J. B. Fuqua, an Atlanta businessman whom we had known since he was in the Georgia State Senate with Jimmy, started one of the first TV stations in Georgia and owned many more. He began going to Emory University for treatment every three or four months to help his depression. For several years he joined with Tom Johnson and Larry Gellerstedt, an Atlanta developer who also struggled with serious depression, to mobilize corporate leaders in Atlanta to include coverage for treatment of mental illnesses in their employees' health insurance benefits. They have made a great impact in the business world in Atlanta and brought important attention to the issue.

Our faith-based communities can also be agents of change and hope. Many people who need mental health services turn first to their clergy for guidance. These spiritual leaders often serve as de facto service providers and can be effective advocates for both treatment and tolerance. It saddens me that I still hear from families and individuals who feel ignored or even ostracized by places of worship when these institutions have so much potential to do good. Just think of how much progress we could make in our campaign to end stigma if the 300,000 congregations in our nation were to truly open their hearts and minds to people with mental illnesses.

During my childhood, the word "cancer" was never spoken out loud. It was a deadly and mysterious disease that was feared, and people suffering from it were shunned. I remember when Jimmy's father was diagnosed in the early 1950s. He had been ill for some time and somehow knew he had cancer, which was confirmed by an exploratory operation. He never asked what the doctors found, however, and until his death, the word was never uttered in his presence. Sometimes people would whisper the word (as if saying it aloud would bring it on) or just call it the "Big C," if they mentioned it at all. Those days are over now, and the way we dealt with cancer seems ridiculous when we reflect on it.

The same should be true of mental illness. "If you look back at the history of diseases, it's clear that when you find causes and treatments, you end stigma," says Kay Jamison, PhD, professor of psychiatry at the Johns Hopkins University School of Medicine, who was diagnosed with bipolar disorder in her twenties and is now one of the country's leading experts on this disease. We now know that mental illnesses are complex brain disorders and that people who have a mental illness cannot help that they have developed the condition. We also now recognize that environmental factors play a powerful role. And finally, we have learned that when people with mental illnesses seek treatment and work on recovery, as Larry Fricks says so eloquently, their "thought processes become healthy." Each of us knows someone like Larry, someone who, as he says, "is striving for a better life." Together we can eliminate stigma and bring a better life within everyone's reach.

2.

THE SCOPE OF
THE PROBLEM

DURING THE 1980 PRESIDENTIAL campaign, I traveled extensively in New Hampshire. I worked hard there, and I talked about mental health at every stop. Hugh Gallen, the governor, was an old friend, and he shared my passion for improving mental health services. One day we visited the state's large public mental health hospital. We were both optimistic that soon the large state hospitals would close and be replaced with community-based services that let people receive treatment and support close to home.

Now, thirty years later, too many people are still living on the streets, leading marginal existences. Millions more simply cannot find the services they need. If help is not readily available, lives are wasted or even lost. In most cases, it is an innocent child, an overwhelmed mother, or a veteran returning from duty who suffers in silence and struggles alone because good mental health care is unavailable. This issue has yet to come to the forefront, even today.

This Is Everyone's Issue

Mental illness does not discriminate.[1] It touches individuals of all ages and knows no geographic, socioeconomic, or ethnic boundaries. Each year almost 60 million adults in the United States suffer from a diagnosable mental disorder.[2] The burden falls most heavily on those who have the most serious mental illnesses, about 13 million adults each year, and their loved ones. This is a problem that hurts every family in our country.

Mental illness is the leading cause of disability in the United States, Canada, and Western Europe, inflicting more damage than cancer, heart disease, or diabetes; it represents a major economic burden to individuals, families, and our society.[3] When measured in lost productive years, depression is the leading cause of disability across all the countries of the world.[4] More young people in this country are disabled by mental illnesses than by accidents, gang violence, drug overdoses, or cancer or diabetes.

Untreated and poorly treated mental illnesses cause untold suffering, exacting a terrible toll on our nation and the world. People with untreated mental disorders have higher absenteeism rates in their jobs. Depression in adults alone accounts for almost 400 million sick days a year in the United States.[5] Cumulatively, adult Americans with mental illnesses—including anxiety disorders, post-traumatic stress disorder (PTSD), and substance abuse disorders—miss a staggering 1.3 billion days of work each year. Serious mental illness was estimated to be associated with a loss of $193.2 billion in personal earnings in the total US population in 2002.[6]

Why are these numbers so overwhelming? Those who live with these illnesses know the answer well. A person with serious clinical depression often suffers from profound sadness and lethargy that can last for weeks or months on end. Sleep patterns and appetite may be turned upside down. Lack of energy and irritability as well as deep despair, hopelessness, and suicidal thoughts are common. This combination of symptoms can make it impossible for an individual to work for extended periods of time, resulting in months or years being lost to this illness.

Of even more devastating impact are the symptoms of schizophrenia. This disease strikes young people in their prime—usually in late adolescence or early adulthood. When Samuel Keith, MD, one of the country's leading experts on schizophrenia, addressed one of our early mental health symposia at The Carter Center, he spoke about the toll that it can take on their lives.

"Schizophrenia," he explained, "is an illness which continues to alter the expectations of two million Americans during the course of their lifetimes. Two million Americans will experience the onset of an illness which will decrease and far too often eliminate the possibility of completing an education, beginning a career, or enjoying a life once filled with such promise. Many will continue an existence without control of that most human of qualities—the human mind and its unique ability to distinguish reality from fantasy, friend from foe, joy from sadness. Yet the two million Americans bearing this diagnosis are far from the only people who have suffered. . . . Each of those [with] schizophrenia has family and friends who care deeply about them and who have suffered, if differently, equally as much. Along with the illness and its private reality of personal and familial suffering and disability comes an enormous cost to our society—a cost compounded by ignorance and fear."[7]

We can calculate the costs of medical care, we can quantify wages lost due to an inability to work, but how do we measure the potential that is lost, the contributions to society that a person with schizophrenia may never make, the pain that must be endured? "'I don't think you understand how bad this illness is,'" said one of Dr. Keith's patients. "'It's like there's a whole world out there, covered with superhighways, with cars and buses and planes and trains, and I just don't have a ticket to ride. . . . I feel like a caterpillar in a cocoon, and I'm never going to be a butterfly.'"[8]

Joel Slack, a nationally recognized mental health consumer advocate and a member of my Mental Health Task Force, lost eight years of productive life to a mental illness that developed when he returned to his hometown after his freshman year at college. He was a basketball star in high school and had been recruited by a major university. But after his first year there, he explained to me, "I came home for the summer and slowly but surely developed a serious psychiatric disability. I had a severe breakdown that landed me in the local hospital. They thought I could overcome the illness at home that summer, but it turned out to be a miserable summer. There was no more discussion about going back to college. I didn't know it back then, but I gave up my dream of ever being a basketball player again. Instead, I was admitted to a long-term psychiatric hospital."

Joel spent the next two and a half years in residential psychiatric hospitals, both private and state funded, and six months in and out of local hospitals. Initially diagnosed with schizophrenia, he lay in a hospital bed for eight months after one breakdown. "My whole system shut down. I couldn't even take care of myself. I had a long beard and was disheveled. The worst thing was I stopped eating. I was extremely fragile." After being released from the hospital, he continued for the next five years to depend on community psychiatric services. "I lived in group homes, and supervised housing, and day treatment programs—the whole gamut."

Even though Joel did go back to college eight years after his initial break, he could no longer play basketball. "The illness, the medication, the institutionalization had taken its toll. So I was left with focusing on academics," he said.

"The initial breakdown and loss of control of your mind is a life-altering experience," he explained. "Terror comes with that loss of control and it's the kind of terror that leaves an imprint on someone's psyche and stays with them for the rest of their lives. I still take medication, not because I'm psychotic anymore but to cover up those remnants of terror that I haven't been able to resolve from years ago."[9] The residual burden that many people carry after a mental illness, the burden of unresolved terror, the anguish, the experiences—these kinds of fear and pain linger on long after the symptoms have been resolved.

A New Hope, for Some

Today, the number of people diagnosed with schizophrenia remains about the same as it was twenty years ago, but the prospects for successful treatment and recovery are quite different. With modern advances in drug therapy and psychosocial care, almost half the individuals who develop schizophrenia can expect to live successfully in the community. With appropriate support and treatment, it is possible to reduce relapses to less than 10 percent.[10]

Elyn Saks, an accomplished professor at the University of Southern California Gould School of Law and a 2009 recipient of the MacArthur Foundation "genius" award, illustrates the potentiality perfectly. Hers is a harrowing story, one that includes hospitalizations and the use of restraints, isolation, and forced treatment. It's also a story that has a very positive outcome because she was able to access many avenues of treatment and support.

When I asked Elyn why she thought she was functioning so well when others were not, she described five pillars that were essential. The first two were good professional help and having the good fortune to respond well to medications. Supportive family and friends were third; an accommodating workplace and work she loved, fourth. The fifth and last she described as "eventually coming to terms with having the illness and needing medication. . . . That took me decades to do."[11]

The prospect of recovery from a serious mental illness like schizophrenia is quite real today if the proper supports are in place, as Elyn's story shows us.[12] But she is one of the lucky few who found ways to get the care and social support she needed. For most, the many barriers to care that exist in our society make it difficult if not impossible to reach for recovery.

Compare Elyn's story with the shocking case of a woman with mental illness that the *Los Angeles Times* recently reported. Two Good Samaritans found her, twenty-two weeks pregnant and wandering the streets "voiceless and naked." They brought her to the emergency room. Her feet and ankles were so filthy it seemed to Mark Morocco, MD, the physician on duty at this Los Angeles hospital, as if she were wearing black boots. He frantically searched for an appropriate place for the woman whom he called "Madonna," but to no avail.

"Our own hospital doesn't deliver babies," Dr. Morocco wrote, "so our psych ward takes no pregnant women past eight weeks. The county evaluation teams wouldn't see Madonna—because she was already at a hospital with psychiatric facilities. The big county psychiatric ERs asked us to fax them the file, and then just didn't respond." Eventually a nurse at the hospital located a phone number for this woman's brother, but Dr. Morocco's elation soon turned to despair: The brother refused to take any responsibility for his sister and simply hung up the phone.[13]

The Access and Quality Chasms

David Satcher, MD, PhD, surgeon general during the Clinton administration and later a member of my Mental Health Task Force, released the first surgeon general's report on mental health in 1999. These reports are used to review major public health problems and make recommendations about what needs to be done to address them. This was truly a breakthrough, and we rejoiced. What a boost to our field to get this kind of attention. The report stated clearly that 80 to 90 percent of the time today we can effectively treat people with mental disorders and enable them to return to full and productive lives.[14] This is truly a very hopeful and positive finding.

Yet despite our scientific knowledge and understanding of what works, numerous studies have documented that the quality of care delivered to people with mental illnesses does not live up to this promise. Each year millions of people do not get the help they require. In addition, there are still vast disparities in the availability of appropriate care depending upon who you are and where you live.

Only 2.5 percent of psychologists in the country are Latino, for example, yet Latinos represent 12.6 percent of the American population today.[15] Access to appropriate care is impossible for many. Among African Americans, similar problems exist. Those with a mental disorder are much more likely to end up in the emergency room than to receive outpatient care. Native Americans and Alaska Natives suffer disproportionately from depression and substance abuse and are also overly represented in inpatient care. Dr. Satcher found that "minority children are much less likely than Whites to get the help they need and much more likely than Whites to be trapped into a system from which many never return."[16] These inequities must be addressed.

We must also do a better job of making the most recent advances and effective treatments available to all who need them. As Philip Wang, MD, DrPH, a psychiatrist and epidemiologist and deputy director of the National Institute of Mental Health (NIMH), explained to me, "It's not like the situation is so hopeless that we don't know how to improve care or help people achieve better outcomes. But there's this impasse where a lot of the innovations—and NIMH pays for many of them, we conduct lots of trials, we show that they're effective—sit on the shelf."[17] In 2005 the Institute of Medicine conducted a major study of the problems that exist in mental health and substance use care. It found that "health care for these conditions—like general health care—frequently is not delivered in ways that are consistent with science, ways that enable improvement and recovery. Moreover, care is sometimes unsafe; more often, it is not delivered at all. This gap between what can and should be and what exists is so large that . . . it constitutes a 'chasm.'"[18]

A significant part of the problem has to do with training. On average, medical students receive only about six weeks of exposure to clinical psychiatry, though 20 percent of medical schools offer as little as three to four weeks. Competition from other departments for curriculum time has also threatened the quality of the students' psychiatric education; and at many schools, the length of rotations is being decreased.[19]

Clinical training may be supplemented by material on behavioral science and neuroscience in other years, but the scope of the material varies widely across medical schools and may or may not be of much relevance in helping new primary care doctors diagnose and evaluate mental disorders once they begin their practices—and that's where most people first turn for help and advice when they have a mental illness.

Another part of the problem is that the mental health care workforce is aging and the federal budget for training new psychiatrists and other mental health professionals is shrinking. The average age of a psychiatrist today is about fifty-seven. Consider the consequences. As sociologist Ronald Manderscheid, PhD, said to me, "That psychiatrist was trained in the Vietnam War era. Tell me how modern that psychiatrist's training is relative to the very best we have now?"[20] At every level, we are failing to invest in training mental health professionals in the most effective techniques available today. This is a very serious, yet solvable problem; we simply have to commit the necessary resources.

Fragmentation of Care

Shortly after the President's New Freedom Commission on Mental Health completed its final report in 2003, we convened our symposium at The Carter Center to discuss its findings. The commission's chair, Michael Hogan, PhD, talked that day about how care delivery has become increasingly complex over the past twenty-five years. The dramatic shift away from large state hospitals to community-based care has created a much more complicated situation. Within the federal government alone there are more than forty programs that might be used by children or adults seeking help. As Mike noted in his remarks, "It is not just that the main problems in mental health care moved from hospitals to communities. . . . If we look deeper, we see major challenges in juvenile justice, in child welfare, in schools, on the streets, and in both public and private disability programs."

What does this mean in real terms? Recently, a friend's twenty-eight-year-old daughter, Trish, was released from a hospital after a major psychotic episode. There was no follow-up care. There was no planning for her future. She had no appointment to meet with a psychiatrist to monitor her medications or follow her progress. One morning, her mother simply received a phone call from the hospital's discharge nurse saying, "We're releasing Trish today. You'd better come over and pick her up or we'll just let her walk out on her own."

Frantic, my friend searched for a residential program for her daughter. "It's as if the right hand doesn't know what the left hand is doing," she said. "If they just let her go, she'd be homeless, out on the street. How would she be able to take her meds? How would she stay safe? I was desperate." Eventually, she found a group home for Trish, but it was forty miles away. Trish surely would have "fallen through the cracks" if her parents had not taken action. She was well enough to be out of the hospital, but not well enough to live on her own.

Fragmentation makes it difficult for people to get effective treatment and achieve good outcomes. This is easy to understand when we look at the patchwork of mental health programs and how they are paid for. The dizzying array includes those administered and funded by state and local mental health agencies, Medicare, Social Security, Supplemental Security Income and other disability payment programs, vocational rehabilitation programs, educational systems, Temporary Assistance to Needy Families, juvenile and criminal justice programs, child welfare agencies, federal block grant programs, and especially Medicaid.

Both children and adults often need services from several different agencies. Some with severe and persistent mental illnesses need not only mental health services, but also housing, education, and employment support, yet there is no coordination among the entities providing these services. Many service providers have expressed interest in the idea of "blending" the funds of the different agencies to coordinate treatments, but officials—local, state, and federal—who administer them don't always make reasonable efforts to coordinate or collaborate and so fragmentation remains a major barrier. Navigating these many systems can be a nightmare.

My own assistant, Lorraine Echols, is a very informed consumer, a mental health advocate, and a member of the Georgia Mental Health Planning and Advisory Council. Her son has a serious mental illness. When he was in grade school, he was punished for his misbehavior and repeatedly suspended. In middle school, the situation got worse. Her insurance didn't cover his treatment adequately. When she sought help from the local community services agency, it would not take her insurance; neither was she eligible for their reduced-rate program. For a short time she was able to place him in a private residential facility on a scholarship. Finally, when she had no way to pay for his treatment, she was forced to place him in the custody of the state Department of Juvenile Justice. Once he turned seventeen, they would no longer pay for his care.

Over the years many dollars have been spent in dealing with his illness, but the services that would help him recover have never been available in a well-organized and effective way.[21]

We who work in the mental health field have always thought that we could do great things if we just had the money. Yet we are now spending approximately $120 billion annually on direct mental health care in our country.[22] And that does not include indirect costs such as housing assistance, supported employment, and lost productivity, to name just a few. But our real problem is not the lack of enough money. Rather, as Dr. Manderscheid told me, it's that "we spend it so poorly. We don't channel it appropriately. A lot of money gets siphoned off."[23] Dr. Manderscheid has spent thirty years working for federal mental health agencies and is one of the country's leading experts on public mental health programs. He explained that because our services and funding sources are so fragmented, so uncoordinated, so complicated, we fall far short of realizing all the benefits we might expect from such a huge investment in mental health.

Insurance Roadblocks

For people in all walks of life, insurance coverage is a major barrier to getting care—if they're lucky enough to have coverage in the first place. Millions of people in the United States do not have coverage. These are people who are working hard but don't earn enough to be able to buy health insurance on the private market. Or their insurance may provide only limited benefits for mental health problems. Those who fall below the federal poverty level can turn to their federal and state governments for help, but we all know these programs are woefully inadequate. And even with the recent efforts to achieve national health care reform, problems still persist.

Insurance companies and policy makers argued for years that covering mental illnesses would "break the bank." This has proven to be false. When I first began working to get employers to provide parity—insurance coverage for mental illnesses that is comparable to that for other illnesses—only a handful of companies did so. That was many years ago, and we learned then that costs do not explode with parity; but we didn't have enough information back then to make a real case.

Today, many companies include mental health coverage with their benefits, and we have plenty of statistics to mount a powerful argument; the best example is the federal government. Since 2001, all federal employees—millions of people— have had a health plan that covers mental health and substance abuse problems just as it does other conditions, and yet the increased cost to the government has been little more than

1 percent when the care is managed.[24] The catastrophic, break-the-bank scenario that insurance companies and their advocates predicted has not materialized.

With the passage of the Paul Wellstone and Pete Domenici Mental Health Parity and Addiction Equity Act in October 2008, another significant milestone was achieved. For the first time, federal legislation mandated that mental health coverage be on a par with physical health benefits. While this represents a great victory for all of us who have been fighting for parity for so long, serious challenges remain. The law only applies to private insurance plans that pay for mental health services; and like many legislative initiatives, its implementation requires writing regulations. There are still many hurdles to overcome before all the financial barriers are removed.

The insurance problem is substantial, but it is not the whole story: People with severe mental illnesses require more than just medical treatment. Many also need a range of social, psychological, and rehabilitative services. We must do more than pay only for "medically necessary" services—medication and hospitalization. The failure to provide for peer support, community residential facilities, and vocational training deprives many people of resources that could contribute to their recovery and independence.

Cultural Barriers

More than thirty years ago I traveled to Tucson with my fellow members of the President's Commission on Mental Health to hear firsthand about problems of access and barriers to care among minorities and people from different ethnic backgrounds. I remember well the story of a woman who had gone to a therapist to confess her fear resulting from her husband's ex-wife having put a hex on her. She was diagnosed as paranoid and prescribed chlorpromazine (Thorazine), an antipsychotic drug. Yet further exploration of her case by a bicultural and bilingual therapist revealed that she was not paranoid at all—and that her dilemma was a very common experience in her culture.

I have been told repeatedly by Latinos that they fear being called "loco" and shaming their families. I also know that many are more reticent to share family problems with a stranger. In a culture where faith and spirituality are strong influences, some interpret their symptoms as deserved punishments for their sins. Low socioeconomic status, separation from family members, and the stresses of immigration and living in a foreign culture can also take a toll. Persons from ethnic and minority groups in our country are less likely to seek outpatient treatment. They are also more likely to have access problems related to being uninsured, underinsured, and living in underserved communities. All these factors make it more difficult for them to get appropriate care.

Why is this so? David C. Henderson, MD, teaches psychiatry at Harvard Medical School. He explained, "We understand that there's an influence of culture in mental illness—how patients communicate, how they manifest symptoms. . . . The classic error arises when residents present a case of a black patient, and they come up with a diagnosis of psychotic disorder based on paranoia. They ask the diagnostic question, 'Do you ever walk down the street and feel like there's somebody out to get you?' That's what we're taught to ask. Typically, the patient will say, 'Yeah.' My message to the residents is, 'Get their address and go walk down their street and then you can understand if it's clinically relevant paranoia or [if] they live on a street that's actually somewhat dangerous.'" Sadly, we do not yet apply what we have learned about the importance of incorporating cultural differences into every aspect of care.

We simply cannot underestimate the importance of a patient's culture. Dr. Henderson went to Cambodia to train primary care doctors in basic psychiatric care, and his experience there provides a dramatic example. He began his psychiatric evaluations by asking patients one of the standard diagnostic questions used in the United States: "Do you hear voices when there is no one in the room?" All the patients said yes. Then he asked the staff and the doctors if they heard voices, and he got the same reply. Finally he asked the minister of health, "Do you hear voices?" Again, the answer was yes. At a meeting on the last day of his visit, the minister of health got up to thank him and then said, "We would like to take the last five minutes to help Dr. David because it seems that he's the only one here who is not in touch with his ancestors."[25] Imagine what is likely to happen if a person from Cambodia comes to an emergency room in our country. He risks being hospitalized as psychotic when in fact he is hearing the voices of his ancestors—he's doing something that is normal for him. Clearly, an understanding of the culture of one's patients is vital if a mental health care provider is to be effective.

John Head, a former journalism fellow at The Carter Center, describes the impact of cultural norms from an African American perspective when he wrote about his own experience with depression in the powerful *Standing in the Shadows*. His courageous description of his own struggles brought much-needed attention to the issue of depression and suicide among African American men.

> More often than not, we lack the communal vocabulary to talk meaningfully about mental illness. In the black community of the small Georgia town where I grew up, someone was either "in his right mind" or had "lost his mind." There were no words for the netherworld in between. . . . The idea that people might be functioning in their day-to-day lives and yet still pay someone to treat their emotional problems was outright bizarre to us. In fact, we thought it was only in the white world that such a thing might happen. "Black folks can't afford to be crazy," we would say.[26]

Alvin Poussaint, MD, professor of psychiatry at Harvard Medical School, has studied this issue in depth and identifies stigma as a critical contributing factor. "There is a wall of silence around mental health issues, particularly around suicide.

Black people today—educated black folks, professionals—will say to you, 'We do not know black people commit suicide.' Others will say, 'Suicide is a white thing.' The black community has suppressed discussion of suicide because of the shame and guilt and stigma attached to it," he explained.[27]

The Need for Better Research

Minorities are seriously underrepresented in mental health research.[28] Scientists are just now coming to understand that medications may affect people of different ethnicities in different ways. We still know far too little about how race and ethnicity affect an individual's reactions to different drugs. Patients may end up either under- or overmedicated. In either case, the outcomes are not good, with the person potentially finding little relief or suffering severe side effects.

These same issues apply in developing better psychological interventions. When researchers do not pay careful attention to real cultural differences in areas such as family structure or use of traditional healers, their research findings may not be valid. Opportunities to provide more effective treatments are lost, and the problem of health disparities remains. To solve this dilemma, it is important that research teams reflect the racial and ethnic mix of the people they are studying. It is time to make this issue a priority in both public and private research efforts.

Geography as a Barrier to Care

While 75 percent of our land mass is considered rural and 17 percent of our population lives there, the needs of rural

Americans are often misunderstood, minimized, and ignored when making mental health policy decisions. People living in rural or geographically remote areas struggle with poor access to care, chronic shortages of mental health professionals, and greater stigma when seeking treatment. They are also more likely to suffer from poverty than those living in cities.

Poverty is a serious problem that compounds the others. There is a strong association between poverty and mental illness, though that relationship is not fully understood. People who are poor are disproportionately diagnosed with more severe disorders. Because of the lack of both early and ongoing care, mental disorders among the poor often become more severe. A vicious cycle develops as an individual with a mental illness becomes even more impoverished and less able to afford care, leading to disastrous consequences.

Mental Illnesses Lead to Premature Death: Part 1

Today in the United States, someone dies by suicide every sixteen minutes; that's more than 30,000 each year. In our country, more lives are lost to suicide than to homicide. Young people between the ages of ten and twenty-four are especially vulnerable. Their rate has doubled in the past four decades and now, ten young lives are lost to suicide every day.[29]

Across all social lines, each person's story is unique. There are many different paths to suicide, but there is one common thread: There are always multiple victims. It is estimated that each suicide produces at least six, and as many as hundreds, of "survivors"—those who are left behind to grieve. Millions of people every year must deal with the tragic consequences. The pain that this engenders can even trigger depression in the survivors. A young woman who attended Emory University in Atlanta and is now an executive at the Coca-Cola Company wrote to me about the aftermath of her brother's suicide.

It has been two and a half years since my brother committed suicide, and I still struggle to say those words, to accept the fact that I will never see him again. There are still times when the phone rings and, for a brief moment, I think it might be him. . . . I still pause when someone asks me if I have siblings; I have yet to come up with a consistent answer. It's a question I don't think I'll ever be fully prepared to answer. I rehearsed all kinds of different responses. To settle on one would only seem to make this surreal experience more concrete. . . .

We all cope with loss in different ways. Through my family's journey to rebuild our lives, I have learned that grief is very personal, and as such, there is no "right way" to deal with the death of a loved one. At first I was incapacitated. My old life seemed almost trivial. The slightest sights, sounds, and experiences would send me spiraling back to the moment I lost my brother. Gradually, the periods of hopelessness that followed these setbacks shortened. I consciously chose to focus on the positives from my brother's life and simply accepted (without dwelling upon) the manner in which it ended.

So much of this pain and grief is preventable, yet we are not implementing what we already know, and every day another ninety-one people will end their lives by suicide.[30] Risk factors for suicide can vary according to age, gender, ethnic group, and occupation, but one thing is certain: Those who suffer from depression are at much greater risk. Studies have shown that more than half of the children and 90 percent of the adults who die by suicide were diagnosed with depression.[31] These statistics cry out for action. Our resource guide provides information on organizations that are developing and disseminating information on a range of prevention programs.

Mental Illnesses Lead to Premature Death: Part 2

Dr. Manderscheid told me that people in the public mental health system die twenty-five years earlier than other people. It is a serious and substantial public health issue. "They don't even get the most rudimentary primary health care that we all take for granted. So if they get high blood pressure, the high blood pressure remains untreated. If they get diabetes, their diabetes remains untreated. If they get chronic heart disease, it remains untreated and they die. That's the starkest contrast I can think of that epitomizes this field."[32]

I wondered whether he was talking about people with severe mental illnesses who were living on the streets.

"No," Ron explained. "These people are actually ongoing clients of state mental health systems around the country. In a certain sense, they're a cut above the people on the street who don't get any care at all. If we actually went out and did research on those individuals, I'm sure they would be worse off than the population I'm talking about. The people we studied are like the canaries in the coal mine. They typify a huge problem. We're literally stealing twenty-five years of their lives because we're not getting appropriate care to them. As an American society, with the wealth we have and the amount of money we spend on health care—$2 trillion a year—and people are literally dying for lack of any care at all, it is a tragedy, a terrible, terrible tragedy."

Ron's research showed that these individuals were dying of natural causes similar to the leading causes of death nationwide: heart disease, cancer, stroke, and respiratory disease.[33] Ron explained that these premature deaths can be attributed to a variety of reasons, such as poor screening, treatment, and follow-up by doctors. Other factors include patients' risky or unhealthy behaviors, such as smoking and poor diet. Still others relate to the impact of poverty, unemployment, or lack of health insurance, conditions that so often afflict those with serious mental illnesses. We know the reasons for this dreadful situation; we can no longer accept the consequences of twenty-five years lost because of our failure to act.

The final report of the 2003 President's New Freedom Commission concluded that our mental health system is not oriented toward helping the people it serves to achieve their single most important goal—recovery. "More individuals could recover from even the most serious mental illnesses if they had access in their communities to treatment and supports that are tailored to their needs."[34] In too many instances, the mental health system ends up working against patients, not for them.

These findings are particularly distressing to me because more than three decades ago, our President's Commission on Mental Health informed Jimmy in its final report that "the one-year study we undertook at your direction has convinced us that a substantial number of Americans do not have access to mental health care of high quality and at reasonable cost. For many, this is because of where they live; for others, it is because of who they are—their race, age or sex; for others, it is because of their particular disability or circumstances." The commission went on to note that there were numerous people with chronic mental illnesses who lacked access to the care they needed, that "thousands who are so disabled receive deplorably inadequate assistance."

In the thirty years since our commission, directed by my longtime friend Thomas E. Bryant, MD, made its assessment of mental health care in the country, so little has changed. Despite the great progress that has been made in understanding the causes of mental illnesses and developing better treatments, we are still struggling against many of the same barriers to care.

Chapter 3

OUR CHILDREN: FALLING
THROUGH THE CRACKS

ALEX RAEBURN WAS HOSPITALIZED after leaving his fifth-grade classroom in a rage. Thus, at the age of eleven, he began a three-year nightmare of repeated hospitalizations, misdiagnoses, and inappropriate treatment before he was finally diagnosed with bipolar disorder. Four years later his younger sister, Alicia, began a similar journey at the age of twelve. These siblings are just two of the millions and millions of children in our country who suffer from serious mental health disorders,[1] the vast majority of whom are unable to find proper care—a situation former surgeon general David Satcher, MD, describes as "a national health crisis."

Alex and Alicia's father, Paul, shared his children's stories with me when he came to The Carter Center as a journalism fellow. In writing about his own experiences, Paul has helped many other parents in similar situations. In one powerful passage he describes the human consequences of this crisis:

> The real tragedy of this neglected epidemic unfolds on lonely, brittle nights, when a child in the grip of a manic outburst runs out of the house toward the street, threatening to jump in front of a passing car. Or when a depressed teenage girl, whom you've already tucked into bed, slips out, quietly takes a bottle of pills from the medicine cabinet and swallows them. Or when parents, doubled over by guilt, call the police to take away a child they can no longer control. Or, most tragically, when a child's suicide attempt is successful.[2]

Today in this country about one-fifth of our children and adolescents have emotional or behavioral problems, and of these, approximately half struggle with conditions that seriously impair their ability to function.[3] The estimates of the number of children affected by serious mental disorders today are about triple the estimates of the early 1990s.[4] While we do not fully understand the reasons for this trend—improved diagnosis, misdiagnosis, a real increase in the problems, or just better reporting—it is alarming.

Mental health problems in children are about as common as broken bones and in many cases as easily addressed. Our failure to treat these problems appropriately has devastating consequences. I have seen adolescents thrown out of school and put in prison when what they needed was help. I have talked with parents who have had to turn their daughter over to the state in order to get her treatment. I have shared the pain of a father who lost his son to suicide.

There is no heated disagreement over the problems. Few on either side of the political or ideological spectrum claim that children and their families are not at risk. Twenty years ago, Lisbeth Schorr wrote a book with a title very similar to mine.[5] It is distressing that the observations made then are still true today. The effects of poverty—fractured families, poor housing and nutrition, limited health care, increased exposure to violence and abuse—all threaten our children and, clearly, the future of our country. We know that mental health is critical to every aspect of a child's growth, physical well-being, and cognitive development. We also know that intervening early to give children a healthy start in life increases their capacity to deal successfully with challenges as they grow up.

Why, then, despite our common understanding of these issues, have we failed to act decisively and powerfully to bring children security and hope? Why is there such apathy about protecting our children? Why isn't there national recognition of the problem and an outcry to provide them with a safe, nurturing environment that enables them to achieve their full potential?

Missed Opportunities:
The Crisis in Access to Care

Despite progress in the field of child and adolescent mental health, millions of young people every year do not get proper help. Only one in five children with a serious emotional disturbance actually uses specialized mental health services.[6] Today, child welfare services, the juvenile justice system, and our schools often provide care to children in need. None of these institutions has as its first priority the delivery of mental health care. In addition, the complexity of promoting collaboration across agency lines of all professionals serving the same child is daunting. All too often there is no cooperation, not enough money, and limited access to trained mental health professionals—and children and their families suffer the tragic consequences.

Schools: Forced to Fill the Gap

Today our schools are expected to fill more and more complicated roles, often with fewer and fewer resources. They are on the front lines when it comes to dealing with mental health issues, yet they are not really prepared to fulfill this role.

Students with emotional and behavioral problems are usually identified and referred to appropriate care by schools only after their teachers can no longer manage them. Many school systems in our nation have few or no psychologists, social workers, or other mental health workers. Because schools often lack the capacity to correctly spot mental or emotional problems early on, children and their families struggle and suffer needlessly, often with disastrous long-term consequences. Nearly seven years may pass from the time parents first begin noticing a problem until the child gets the proper treatment.[7] We can and we must do better.

Mark Weist, PhD, director of the Center for School Mental Health at the University of Maryland School of Medicine in Baltimore, has been working for the last ten years to find ways to address the problems of a mental health system that is not adequately reaching kids in need and a school system that has to cope with the consequences. Mark and his team are focusing on finding new ways to bring together the mental health and educational communities to embrace a common goal: reducing both academic and nonacademic barriers to learning. Every parent who has watched a child dealing with depression or anxiety knows that the child's academic performance suffers. By addressing mental health concerns, we also improve school performance.

Great things can happen when we are willing to make the investment to provide high-quality programs. For example, the Los Angeles Unified School District has developed an innovative program to help multiracial, multicultural, and bilingual children who have been exposed to a wide variety of traumatic events.[8] This program uses a cognitive-behavioral approach that has been widely tested and studied and shown to ease the symptoms of trauma and build coping skills and resiliency in children—an excellent way to prevent mental illnesses. This translates into measurable improvements in school performance, including better attendance and behavior in the classroom. This program has been successful with children from all kinds of backgrounds and is a model for many communities.

The Special Problem of
Children in Foster Care

Children in foster care are especially vulnerable; they have already been exposed to trauma by virtue of being brought into the protective services system in the first place. Approximately 800,000 children are reported to be in the foster care system nationwide at any one time,[9] and a staggering number of them have mental illnesses. Stephen Hornberger, MSW, who was the director of behavioral health for the Child Welfare League of America, tells me that anywhere from 40 to 85 percent of kids in foster care have mental health disorders. These children use mental health services much more often than other children in the Medicaid system, which is a major payor for these services.

During The Carter Center's twentieth annual mental health symposium in 2004, a panel of young people from Atlanta talked about their problems growing up. One participant was Angela, a poised young woman in medical school who was also working at the Georgia Parent Support Network as a peer mentor. "My life in foster care began when I was 6 years old," she told us.

My mom did not want me. For years I said that it was because she was very young. Before then, when I was still at home, it was like I played the mother role to my siblings. When I left my mom to live in a foster home, I was very, very upset because nobody told me why I left. They could not tell me anything. I was 6, so if they had said anything, I would not have understood it. I have been in different foster homes and group homes. I have been in mental institutions. . . .

It was really hard growing up, having to fight in different group homes and foster homes. One of the things that used to bother me the most was one of the girls always got to go home on holidays, and I wished I had a family that I could go home to. That used to eat me up inside so much.[10]

Youth like Angela still face many problems once they are in foster care: high turnover among state social workers, budget cuts that often limit access to services, Medicaid options that offer insufficient mental health care, and logistical and emotional difficulties if they are moved from one home to another or have to change families or schools multiple times.

Families who take in foster children also must deal with this complicated and imperfect system. One family I learned about in Massachusetts adopted three children from foster care. All developed serious mental and emotional problems that required intensive and targeted treatment. The family's private insurance paid for only six mental health visits a year per child, and the public programs were totally inadequate. At different points, they were compelled to surrender custody of each of the three children to the state Department of Social Services in order to get them the care they needed—a situation biological parents sometimes face as well.[11]

The problems in our foster care system are multiple, complex, and well documented. Yet we also know, as Angela's story illustrates so well, that children have an enormous capacity to deal with adversity and that with proper help, they can be amazingly resilient. This undeniable fact makes it all the more disturbing that we have yet to adequately address the persistent problems that plague our foster care system and cause so many children such terrible suffering.

Diagnostic Difficulties

Today, pediatricians are usually the first and often the only professionals offering care; they prescribe most of the medications and often counsel families and their children.[12] It stands to reason, then, that parents and pediatricians should be on the same page. But when it comes to a child in need, studies have shown that those looking out for the best interests of a child can have difficulty communicating effectively about mental health issues.[13] This is particularly distressing because the identification of children's mental health problems hinges on good dialogue between parents and doctors.

Even when things go smoothly, referrals from pediatricians to mental health specialists often mean three- to four-month delays before the child is seen.[14] But that is not the worst of it. More than half of the children who are sent to specialists for treatment never actually set foot in their offices.

Why does this happen? There is a serious shortage of skilled clinicians; many professionals who do specialize in mental health have not been adequately trained in the most up-to-date and effective practices; many children are in settings that can only respond to crises, often in an uncoordinated and wholly inadequate way; mental health care inequities in both public and private insurance programs make it difficult for many families to afford appropriate care; and stigma remains a huge problem. Parents are fearful that their children will be labeled, or they may struggle with shame and denial themselves. Paul Raeburn told me that he initially delayed treatment for his son "because I was not going to be the parent of a mentally ill kid."

Obtaining an accurate diagnosis can be complicated, particularly for those with the most serious mental and emotional problems. We still do not have tools like x-rays, ultrasounds, or blood tests for diagnosing mental illnesses.

Doctors have to base their diagnoses on the child's symptoms, which can sometimes present significant difficulties. In many cases, symptoms of different disorders are similar. In others, they vary over time; and children, especially young ones, may have trouble accurately describing what is going on. Timothy Wilens, MD, associate professor of psychiatry at Harvard Medical School and an expert in the challenges of diagnosing children, notes that "Each human being carries a unique set of experiences and vulnerabilities that combine to make the person more or less susceptible to psychiatric disorders. Some of these factors are environmental, some biological, and most a complex interplay of the two." [15] He goes on to explain that in order to diagnose and treat a problem effectively, the doctor needs to understand the interaction among all of these factors as deeply as possible, which is often a complex task requiring input "from those who know the child best—the child's parents." Dr. Wilens also acknowledges that the process can be a lengthy one of trial and error.

Parents play an important role in achieving an accurate diagnosis, but even with their best efforts, problems can still occur. I know this from my own experience. Friends often turn to me for advice when their children encounter difficulties. Mark, the teenage son of a family I know well, had begun to isolate himself, losing interest in activities he had once enjoyed, like baseball and soccer. His parents worried about him because he seemed sad, but when they asked if anything was bothering him, he always said, "Oh, I'm fine."

One day, a neighbor found Mark at home alone, crying. He told her, "Something must be wrong with me; I'm never happy anymore." The friend wanted to tell his parents because she thought he might need to see a doctor. But he said, "I don't want them to know." So she didn't tell them, but because she knew I had worked on mental health issues, she told me, and I told them.

I don't know how long the parents would have waited to get help for Mark, but when I confirmed their suspicions, they immediately took him to a mental health professional, the only one in their small town. Over a period of months, the clinician worked with Mark to try to get an accurate diagnosis. This required changing his medication frequently, with varying consequences and disturbing side effects. Some caused him to want to sleep all the time; others made him extremely agitated. For a long while it seemed that nothing worked. Finally, after many months and consultation with another mental health professional, Mark was correctly diagnosed with depression and prescribed the right treatment. Now he is back in school and doing well.

Because the symptoms of severe mental illnesses often overlap, clinicians may differ on the type of illness a child has, and the latest research can sometimes lead to more confusion. This is dramatically illustrated in the controversy surrounding the diagnosis of bipolar disorder in young children. Up until the early 1990s, it was thought that this illness did not develop until adolescence. Then, in 1995, two child psychiatrists at Massachusetts General Hospital, Janet Wozniak, MD, and Joseph Biederman, MD, published an influential paper reporting that some young patients suffered from mania.[16] This discovery led them to conclude that there was a childhood version of bipolar disorder. In the years since, the number of children treated for bipolar disorder has increased, but some professionals have raised concerns about our ability to accurately diagnose this condition. Gabrielle Carlson, MD, director of child and adolescent psychiatry at Stony Brook University School of Medicine in New York, has worked on this issue for years and believes we are overdiagnosing children with bipolar disorder. Is the rise in the number of children identified with bipolar disorder due to better diagnostic techniques or the opposite—mistaken diagnoses? I do not know—perhaps no one can answer this question at this time.

What I do know is that for too many parents, it is still extremely difficult to find a clear path toward helping a child who is emotionally troubled.

The Medication Controversy

The issue of medicating children with mental health problems is complex: Some families swear by their children's medications, but others believe that the medical treatment of serious mental and emotional disturbances has led to excessive and harmful uses of drugs. Complicating matters is that there has been very limited research on how antidepressants and other psychiatric drugs affect the developing minds of young children. In many instances we do not fully know what the impact of the drugs really is. While the volume of medications prescribed for children has increased steadily over the past two decades, most studies on the effects of these drugs pertain only to adults.

This problem gave rise to concerns regarding a slight increase in suicidal thoughts among children taking antidepressants. In response, the US Food and Drug Administration (FDA) directed manufacturers to inform users of this with a "black box warning" on their packaging—the most severe warning of risk the FDA requires—and advised physicians to monitor children on these medications once a week for the first month of treatment. These restrictions and the publicity surrounding the study created fear and uncertainty about what to do. Peter Jensen, MD, president of the REACH Institute in New York City and head of adolescent and child psychiatry at the Mayo Clinic, explained the nuances of the controversy to me: "It appears that the risk for suicide might have been overstated, and we may have underappreciated the risk for deaths due to depression itself. Now people are worried that the backlash may have been too strong and has actually resulted in more harm than good."[17]

Advances in Our Understanding of Serious Mental Illnesses in Children

Mary Jane England, MD, an old friend, trained as a child psychiatrist but practiced for only a decade in the late 1960s and early 1970s before she stopped seeing patients and pursued a career in policy and advocacy. I often wondered why she had decided to change career paths, and one day I asked. "There was so little we could do to help children struggling with serious mental and emotional problems back then," she told me. "We just didn't know what worked and had few tools to successfully intervene." In those days, many children with serious conduct disorders were simply described as "delinquent" or "problem" kids and got shuffled around from one agency to another. There was no system of care.

We have made great progress over the last thirty years in our understanding of mental illnesses in childhood. One of the most exciting areas of research focuses on their biological roots. We now know that all serious mental illnesses—schizophrenia, bipolar disorder, depression, and anxiety disorders— are types of brain disorders. We also know that the development of these diseases is influenced by a variety of social and psychological factors during the early years of life. Fifty percent of all major mental illnesses start in children before the age of fourteen, and 75 percent, including substance abuse, are known by the age of twenty-four. Most of the childhood disorders extend into adulthood, and most of the adult illnesses we are working with today have their roots in childhood.[18]

Elaine Walker, PhD, of Emory University, has been studying the development of schizophrenia in individuals for many years. She began by collecting childhood home movies of people who had been diagnosed with this disorder, and in them she observed that as these youngsters crawled and toddled, they moved their arms and legs and hands in subtly abnormal ways. They also seemed uncomfortable and irritable and expressed negative emotions such as anger and disgust more frequently than their siblings.

"These are subtle things," she explained to me. "Not so severe that a parent would say, 'Oh my God, there is something wrong with my child!' But they suggest that the brain abnormalities that create the vulnerability to this devastating illness may be present even at birth."

Dr. Walker and her colleagues built upon their early work to find out what causes children born with a genetic predisposition to develop schizophrenia later in life. She and other investigators have now concluded that the teenage years are the critical risk period for the onset of this disorder because developmental changes that are occurring in the brain at that time interact with inborn vulnerability. They are currently studying ways to identify those who are most likely to develop schizophrenia so that we may begin their treatment early in life.[19]

Dr. Walker's research opens a small window into our understanding of how and why these disorders develop. It raises the possibility of creating better interventions for children at risk and is just one example of the great progress that has been made in understanding and addressing mental illnesses in children. There are now proven treatments for the millions afflicted with serious childhood disorders. New medications can be very helpful and can complement psychotherapy conducted by skilled clinicians.

Outcomes improve when a system of care is implemented with the child and family as the primary focus. A system of care coordinates and integrates the activities of all agencies involved with the child and eliminates harmful or inefficient barriers. In more than 40 states, these kinds of programs exist, but only on a limited basis. Our failure to make them available to all families is a national disgrace.[20]

Preventing More Serious Problems Later in Life

Ensuring that all children have access to effective treatment is absolutely essential. Lost opportunities to promote healthy development are difficult to regain, and without a solid start in life, youngsters are at much greater risk for serious disability and even death as they grow up. At our 2008 symposium, the late Jane Knitzer, EdD, talked eloquently about the need to act decisively to improve children's mental health, elaborating on the findings of a new study by the National Center for Children in Poverty.[21]

When mental health problems in children are identified early, we can intervene and interrupt a downward spiral. Screening is best accomplished in settings where children spend the most time, such as in schools, or where they visit regularly, such as the pediatrician's office. Symptoms are more likely to be caught early in these trusted settings, but unfortunately, in so many cases this is not done.

In 2008 a major study on preventing mental, emotional, and behavioral disorders in children was released, documenting the remarkable progress that has been made in the last fifteen years. It highlighted the window of opportunity that exists between early symptoms and the onset of a full-blown mental disorder and stressed the need to intercede in this critical period—to make prevention a regular part of care for children, just as we do for their physical health. There are many effective programs available.

Some are preventive in nature, aimed at young people in general and designed to promote good mental health by addressing major risk factors. Primary schools use the Good Behavior Game. Studies have shown that it significantly reduces aggressive and disruptive behavior in the first grade. It also has benefits over the longer term, lowering the risk of alcohol and drug abuse and reducing the likelihood that highly aggressive boys develop more serious disorders as adults.

Others focus on specific groups, such as adolescents at

risk for depression. Several studies have demonstrated that teaching them to cope with stress has prevented more serious episodes of depression.

Enhancing parenting skills can also improve a child's mental health and behavior. The Positive Parenting Program includes a television series on how to handle common child-rearing problems, and in-person skills training teaches how to handle aggressiveness or lack of cooperation. These interventions have lowered disruptive behaviors and the effect lasts over time.[22]

Fostering Resiliency

Some people say that resiliency, the ability to succeed in the face of daunting adversity, is an inborn trait—either you are born with this kind of strength or you are not. But others believe, as I do, that whether or not you have this innate tendency, resiliency can be nurtured and fostered.

Carl Bell, MD, a member of my Mental Health Task Force and president and CEO of the Community Mental Health Council, is one of the field's foremost advocates for promoting resiliency in children. He speaks passionately about the need to shift our focus from a deficit-based model of child development, where the goal is to overcome problems, to a strength-based model that emphasizes support. Carl puts it this way: "Most of life is about attitude and perception." Children are best served when we help them develop the skills they need to frame whatever challenges and obstacles they may meet in a positive paradigm.

Carl has identified a number of characteristics present in resilient children—the same characteristics that enabled Angela to overcome her troubled childhood. These include having a sense of purpose in life, confidence in one's ability to control any given situation, compassion for others, a belief in the fundamental goodness of people, and the energy and resourcefulness to make things happen. John Gates, PhD, former director of the Mental Health Program at The Carter Center, describes them as "characteristics that enable children to work well, play well, love well, and expect well."

We now know a great deal about how to nurture resiliency in children. Carl talks about "creating social fabric around children." John describes it as the need for "stable support from caretakers." When I was growing up in Plains, I took these things for granted. Everyone knew everyone else in town. Church and school were the centers of our community and strong and positive influences on my life and those of my siblings and friends. So much has changed since then, and in too many communities across our country the social fabric I took for granted no longer exists. Too many children are left to struggle with a whole host of stressful circumstances— violence, divorce, poverty, and war, to mention just a few— without effective supports. We can and must do more.

An innovative program called Check and Connect, developed by the University of Minnesota, uses strategies such as social skills training and relationship building to intervene in student engagement with school, reduce dropout rates, and increase school completion. The program was initially designed to meet the needs of students with behavioral and learning challenges by pairing students with a patient, caring adult mentor. Studies have demonstrated over and over the positive effects achieved by this program, yet because of funding constraints it remains only a demonstration project.[23]

Why is it that we are so slow to take what we know works and make it available to communities all across the country? Historically, little money has been allocated for prevention programs or those that build on children's strengths.[24] Multiple environmental factors have been proven to nurture a healthy mind. Protective factors such as social inclusion and a sense of positive self-esteem can be promoted to positively influence a child's development.[25] Enhancing a child's learning ability, self-confidence, and interpersonal skills are the wisest investments we can make. Failing to support programs that do so is thoughtless and shortsighted. All of us benefit when a child is healthy and able to learn and succeed in school. And all of us suffer when children lose their way.

Not a Moment to Waste

We are all familiar with the adage "A stitch in time saves nine." When it comes to children with mental illnesses, this proverb couldn't be more apt. If budding issues are not adequately addressed early on, they become bigger and more often devastating problems later in life. Our inattention is causing unnecessary pain, trauma, and death. The wasted potential is immeasurable.

A wealth of research demonstrates that mental health

problems during childhood are often precursors to delinquency, substance use, smoking, risky sexual behavior, and school failure. Studies have found that children in the first grade with a combination of hyperactivity and social problem-solving deficits have a greatly increased rate of drug and alcohol use when they reach the ages of eleven or twelve, which can lead to a variety of other antisocial behaviors and problems.[26] When childhood disorders are not treated early, they can spawn poor employment opportunities and poverty in adulthood. Kathryn Power, MEd, director of the Center for Mental Health Services at the federal Substance Abuse and Mental Health Services Administration, summed it up this way at a Carter Center symposium: "Untreated childhood disorders can close the door on a lifetime of opportunities."[27] Indeed, in the most tragic cases, untreated problems may ultimately end in death.

As I reflect on all that I have learned and all the changes that have taken place in the field of children's mental health over the past thirty years, I am struck by the wisdom of another great child advocate, the former president of the John D. and Catherine T. MacArthur Foundation, Adele Simmons, who summarized the challenges we face today: "We have gone beyond merely cataloguing problems to a relatively sophisticated understanding of what causes them. We know a fair amount about points of intervention and how to intervene. We know what can go wrong when children do not have confidence in their future, feel they do not belong, and are devalued. We have seen success in repairing damaged children, especially in early childhood. We know what to do, but there are not enough mental health professionals for every troubled young person or family in this country. We need an infrastructure that can take the knowledge that the mental health field has acquired and apply it nationwide. We need to establish better partnerships between mental health professionals and education and church and community leaders, business people and parents, local and federal governments. We cannot accept the status quo."[28]

And we cannot delay, for as my good friend and our nation's surgeon general while we were in the White House, the late Dr. Julius Richmond, observed, "Every day that we do not intervene with effective programs, we are losing remarkable human potential. And every child whose potential is wasted is an incredible loss to the nation."[29]

4.

LOOKING AFTER
OUR ELDERLY

MY MOTHER USED TO say that she thought times had changed more in her lifetime than in any previous generation. She lived a few miles outside of Plains, where we now live, in a big farmhouse surrounded by a fence to keep out the bears. She remembered playing in the yard one day when she heard a terrible noise. She climbed on the fence to see what it was, and something big was coming down the road. It turned into her yard, and she was too afraid to get down from the fence, so she just stood there and cried until her father came and got her. The "something" was an automobile. Someone was sick and the doctor had been called.

Things have changed dramatically in my lifetime, too. When I was a child, we had an outhouse in the backyard, a barn with one cow that my two brothers took turns milking, and a few pigs. Our father was very strict and we did our best to please him. One day, when it was Murray's turn to take the cow to graze by the side of Daddy's garage, a car passed, frightening the cow. It ran the whole long block home down the middle of the dirt street, dragging Murray the last part of the way. When Mother asked him why he didn't just turn the rope loose, he said, "I couldn't. Daddy told me not to."

Times were hard back then and not only for us, for everybody. Looking back, I realize how concerned our parents and neighbors were about our health. Contagious diseases spread rapidly; my brothers, little sister, and I all had measles, whooping cough, mumps, and chicken pox. It was always a big relief when these diseases were behind us, because they were bound to happen and they often led to complications and sometimes even death.

Times were different in other ways, too. Families were closer, and extended families included widowed parents and grandparents. My grandmother's mother was always there when I was little and visited my grandparents. I have memories of her sitting by the fireplace in a rocking chair, shelling peas or crocheting, doing something useful. Years later when my grandmother died, my grandfather, Papa, came to live with us. My father had died the year before, and Papa helped mother with the farm, with caring for us children, and with doing odd jobs around the house.

Recently, Jimmy and I rode our bikes out of town to my mother's old home place, which is now our farm. We walked for a while and came to the family cemetery where my ancestors are buried. The birth dates on some of the grave markers go back to the 1700s. We noticed that few of these early settlers had reached what we would now call a "ripe old age." Several had died within a period of a few weeks, and I remembered my mother telling me that dysentery had taken their lives. There was the grave of a sixteen-year-old girl who had died from burns when her clothes caught fire as she stood before an open fire. And it was particularly sad to see so many tiny graves of infants and to think about how many children in those days had died at birth or in the first months of life.[1]

Conditions have changed greatly from what I remember as a child, thanks to improved sanitation, widespread immunization, and wonder drugs. Healthier lifestyles have played a role, too, as we've learned more about the benefits of improved diets and physical fitness. Life expectancy in our country at the turn of the twentieth century was forty-seven. In 2000, it reached seventy-seven and will continue to increase as the post–World War II baby boomers age.[2]

As Robert Butler, MD, an expert on aging with whom I worked when Jimmy was president, says, "We are in the middle of a revolution: the longevity revolution. In less than a century, we have gained more in life expectancy than in the preceding fifty centuries."[3] The longevity revolution is indeed a reality, and with it has come many new challenges for our society.

These Issues Hit Close to Home

My interest in the needs of elderly people, especially as they intersect with mental health issues, began as I campaigned for Jimmy. I visited many senior citizen centers, convalescent hospitals, and nursing homes. Some of the places were cheery, with people enjoying crafts, storytelling, or music, but others were somber, with too many expressionless people sitting slumped over in their chairs.

In a nursing home at one campaign stop, I met three men playing cards. I asked them about their earlier lives. One had been a college president, the second an English professor, and the third a medical doctor. "We do the same thing every day," they told me. "Play cards and feel useless."

Toward the end of my mother's life, when she lived in an assisted living facility, mental health issues for elderly people took on a new urgency for me. So many in my mother's facility could have benefited from psychiatric help, but for most of them the option of receiving professional care was never even considered.

My mother had been forced to retire from her job at the Plains post office on her seventieth birthday, in 1975. I came back home from a campaign trip and my brother told me she had been crying all week. Trying to cheer her up, I said, "Mother, you've had to get up and be at the post office at seven o'clock every morning for as long as I can remember. Isn't it going to be wonderful to be able to stay home and sleep late and be leisurely for a change?"

"It's not that," she replied. "It's just that no one thinks I can do good work anymore." She was as distressed as those three professional men who felt they no longer led meaningful lives.

Everyone ages differently. For some people, the memories and activities of a life well lived add zest and energy and a sense of anticipation even into the golden years. But for others, there is little but loneliness, emptiness, regret, infirmity, and despair. Depression can be one's constant companion. The statistics tell the story: About 11 percent of adults older than 70 have some form of depression.[4]

Our President's Commission on Mental Health found that many elderly people suffered from significant mental health problems but few received treatment. Part of the reason, we found, was that often they were told, and many believed, that the symptoms of mental disorders are natural parts of growing old.

Many still believe that depression is just a normal part of aging. But we know this is wrong. People can find great pleasure in life even if they are "elderly." Jimmy and I have led active lives for years. We have been blessed with good health that allows us to travel and to continue working on our programs. But our circumstances are extraordinary.

Despite losses, other members of our family also have had successful old ages. Jimmy's mother, Miss Lillian, joined the Peace Corps at the age of sixty-eight. The advertisements to join had the words "Age no barrier," and she believed them. And even my mother found a new life after her forced retirement. Following a period of grieving for her old role, she started working part-time at the flower shop in Plains, and for many years thereafter felt happy that she was making a contribution to her community.

I have seen time and again that elderly people can recover from emotional setbacks and go on to have fulfilling lives. We know from experience that the "golden years" can be golden. We don't have to resign ourselves to late-life depression by accepting the idea that it is just part of what happens when one gets old.

Depression in Older Adults

Though most of us older adults have the capacity to remain mentally healthy, millions of Americans over age sixty-five suffer from mental disorders, including Alzheimer's disease, depression, and anxiety disorders. In addition, many experience symptoms such as difficulty sleeping, loneliness and social isolation, fear of abandonment, and drug misuse. Many of these problems can be accurately diagnosed and treated. Unrecognized and untreated, however, they can be particularly debilitating for older adults.

Depression is one of the most common of these disorders, and it can be dangerous for older people, since so few seek treatment. Fewer than 3 percent of older adults receive outpatient mental health treatment from specialty providers, and only 30 percent of older adults who live in the community and need mental health services actually get help.[5] Untreated depression can worsen dementia and suppress the immune system.[6] It can cause or aggravate other medical illnesses. For instance, it is a risk factor for heart attack. And for those who have had a heart attack, the likelihood of having another is greater if they are depressed.[7] Depression can also be brought on by a heart attack or a diagnosis of cancer, by a stroke or another serious illness. It often co-occurs with these illnesses and can worsen their outcomes. People who are depressed have a much harder time following doctors' orders and taking good care of themselves, further increasing their disability.

Late-life depression is the leading cause of suicide among elderly people. The incidence of suicide shoots up dramatically after retirement age, accounting for 25 percent of all suicide attempts each year, and white men ages sixty-five years or older have the highest suicide rate in America.[8] Ninety percent of those who die by suicide have at least one diagnosable mental or substance abuse disorder.[9] This is a stubborn problem, one that is often the result of a lack of recognition of the real illness and misdiagnosis. Research has found that one-third of older men saw their primary care physician in the week before dying by suicide. Seventy percent saw their physicians within the prior month.[10] Just think of the lives that might have been saved if their illness had been properly diagnosed and treated.

Why Is Depression So Prevalent in This Age Group?

What can bring on depression in older people? Deteriorating health is often experienced as a profound loss. Even simple tasks may become much more difficult to perform when one is ill or disabled, and the increasing caregiving responsibilities that accompany such decline can also become discouraging and burdensome for a spouse and family.

Forced retirement and job loss are heavy blows, especially

for men, who may experience the diminished income, relative isolation, and boredom of retirement as a loss of purpose. Financial difficulties in the face of lost resilience and fewer opportunities can cause despair. Isolation, of course, comes in many forms: The death of a spouse or dear friend may disrupt one's life and leave one lonely; memory, eyesight, and hearing begin to fail, intensifying the sense of being alone; the move to a nursing facility or relative's home in order to be cared for safely can cause disruption and disorientation. Isolation is one of the most debilitating of the late-life experiences.

But perhaps one of the most pervasive yet invisible forces is "ageism," a term coined by Bob Butler in 1969.[11] It refers to the stereotypic and often negative bias against elderly adults. In America, we don't revere our elders as valued members of our communities, as many other societies do. In our culture, older people are often marginalized and left to feel useless and unimportant. Many experience discrimination because of the stereotypes that they are childish, stubborn, and needy. As with other stereotypes, this is untrue and leads to a great waste of human talent, wisdom, and experience.

Care for Older People with Depression Is Lacking

Jürgen Unützer, MD, a nationally recognized researcher in providing care to people with late-life depression, asserts that primary care doctors diagnose only about 50 percent of the cases of depression that come before them. This means that half the people who walk into their doctor's office with major depression are not diagnosed.

Why are so many cases missed? In a study from Texas A&M University that videotaped patients' visits to their primary care doctors, a research team led by Ming Tai-Seale, PhD, MPH, found that mental health issues came up in 22 percent of the visits, but that conversations about them typically lasted only two minutes.

Time wasn't the only factor here. One of the most discouraging interactions was the following:

> **Patient:** I've just been crying my eyes out.
> **Doctor:** Why?
> **Patient:** I don't know. People ask me how I am, I just cry.
> **Doctor:** Oh, well. I am not going to ask you that anymore.

In summarizing this research, Dr. Tai-Seale explained that while there were exceptions, overall, mental health was only infrequently assessed, physicians had poor knowledge of psychiatric medications, and they offered patients little empathy even when it was clear they were in distress.[12]

The shortage of physicians adequately trained in geriatric care goes a long way to explain why elderly people who are depressed do not get the treatment they need. Primary care doctors struggle against many constraints imposed by the demands of their profession—constant pressure to improve productivity, inadequate insurance even from Medicare, time-consuming reporting and record-keeping. These factors make it difficult for even the most caring primary care doctor to have sufficient time to recognize and properly treat what is a very common ailment among older patients. This means that few are referred to mental health specialists even when they show symptoms of severe depression.[13] It may even explain why the suicide rate is so high in men over age sixty-five, despite the fact that such a large percentage of them visited their doctors in the weeks before their deaths. Their symptoms were not recognized or attended to.

The delicate balancing act often required for effective treatment with antidepressants can pose other problems. For most people with depression—young or old—finding the right medication in the correct dose is a long process that requires medical skill, patience, good communication between doctor and patient, and several adjustments in dosage or medication. In addition, an elderly patient may have other confounding medical issues such as dementia, dizziness, brain damage from strokes, or prescriptions for other ailments that make careful and frequent monitoring for drug interactions necessary. This is best accomplished by a psychiatrist or, better yet, a geriatric psychopharmacologist, a physician who is highly skilled in dealing with older people taking psychiatric medications. But how many communities have such specialized professionals? The answer is very few. Not enough medical students are going into this field to cover the growing ranks of aging patients, and mismanagement of medications is a very serious problem for millions of older people.

There is an urgent need for doctors who have been properly trained in the problems and processes of aging. Nationwide, the Institute of Medicine says there are only 7,100 doctors certified in geriatric care—one for every 2,500 Americans over the age of seventy. They estimate the country will need an additional thirty thousand doctors trained in the field to meet the needs of the aging baby-boomer population.[14] Achieving that goal doesn't look possible at the current pace, according to a recent report by the Public Policy Institute, an independent research association. Only 3 of the nation's 145 medical schools have full-time programs in geriatrics. Less than 3 percent of all medical students take even one course in this specialty, according to the report.[15]

Many seniors are quick to tell a story or two about doctors who don't understand the issues of aging—or who don't take the time to hear them out. "Most of them want you out [of the exam room] in five minutes," said Jack Myers, eighty-one, a Torrance, California, resident who recently went through three physicians before finding a primary care doctor he liked. "You start getting all these creaks; it's scary getting old. You want someone to spend a little time with you."[16] Our current health care system makes this very difficult for doctors to do.

That some elder patients feel ashamed about having a mental disorder compounds the problem. They may be afraid of getting treatment or of even acknowledging that they have a mental illness. They may worry that if they say they need mental health services, they will jeopardize their health care and their insurance. They may also be afraid they will lose financial security and their independence. They may believe that they risk embarrassment, isolation, or being declared incompetent. At worst, they may fear institutionalization, being sent away somewhere and never being heard from again.[17]

Further complicating matters is that older generations have been taught not to depend on others to take care of them, and very few want to be treated by a psychiatrist. The referral system doesn't work very well, so if a general practitioner does do all the right things—recognizes that the patient is depressed, spends time talking with him or her, and finally gives a referral to a mental health professional—the patient still may not go.

A Hopeful Model

In the largest treatment trial for late-life depression to date, a project called IMPACT (Improving Mood: Promoting Access to Collaborative Treatment for Late-Life Depression), researchers followed 1,801 older adults with depression for two years.[18] Researchers found a 50 percent or greater improvement in depression in the treated patients after twelve months, compared to those who received the usual care.

What made this program so successful? Each participating clinic had a "depression care manager," a nurse, social worker, or psychologist who educated patients diagnosed with a mental illness and monitored their responses to the antidepressants prescribed by the primary care providers. The care manager also coached patients in developing positive thoughts and behaviors and offered a brief course of counseling that included a plan for what to do in case of relapse. In more severe or stubborn cases, a psychiatrist was called in to consult on the case and work with the care team. The program, developed by Jürgen Unützer, MD, at the University of Washington, actually saves money while it cures depression. Pharmacy costs go down, and the costs of other outpatient services and mental health services also decrease with the use of on-site mental health care managers.[19]

The Emotional Costs of Caregiving

When a family member becomes ill, the whole family suffers. I know this from experience. When I was thirteen, my father died. He was sick for only about six months, but our family life changed dramatically. I was the oldest of four children, and to help Mother, it was my responsibility to care for my two younger brothers and my little sister, who was only four years old. I remember sitting on the floor by my father's bed, studying my lessons. I prayed and prayed and clung to the thought that my father would get well.

But he didn't get well, and after he died, my mother, an only child who had been a full-time homemaker, had to go to work.

Less than a year after my father's death, an early morning telephone call came. I heard my mother scream and went running to see what had happened. Her mother had died. We children crowded around her, and we all cried. How could this have happened? Mama hadn't even been sick. We were all distraught, and over the coming weeks, we consoled each other. Papa was especially devastated. He tried to stay at home in his big farmhouse but was miserable. Within a few months of Mama's death, he left the farm—the only home he'd ever known—and moved in with us. He was seventy then, and he lived to be ninety-five. These experiences made a deep impression on me and certainly colored how I dealt with my mother's final years.

The family caregiver is the backbone of our country's long-term, home-based, community care system. But the strains that providing this care puts on our society and on these individuals are quite apparent, and the emotional costs are high.[20] Many caregivers experience a limited social life; infringement on privacy; sleep deprivation; chronic emotional and physical fatigue; marital conflict; and feelings of anger, grief, guilt, resentment, and hopelessness. Family caregivers are at risk for a wide range of problems related to their physical and mental health, finances, employment, and retirement. They are not trained to deliver complicated care, treated as partners in the patient's care, or encouraged to maintain their own good health.[21] All of this can lead to caregiver burnout and depression, especially among elderly caregivers who may have fewer internal resources to draw upon.

The needs of family caregivers have been a priority of mine for many years. The Rosalynn Carter Institute for Caregiving (RCI) at Georgia Southwestern State University, near my home in Sumter County, is doing groundbreaking work supporting Americans who are in challenging caregiving roles.[22] One of their priorities is helping the spouses of people with Alzheimer's disease and other forms of dementia. The RCI has identified innovative programs that offer concrete advice on how to deal with difficult behaviors like wandering, repeatedly asking questions, and agitation. They also focus on the importance of taking care of oneself, as well as teaching quick and easy ways to better manage stress. In Georgia, as well as at demonstration sites across the country, the institute's projects are helping older people who are at high risk themselves to stay mentally healthy and to more effectively support their disabled loved ones.

The Doubly Stigmatized

Not only do older individuals struggle with the symptoms and consequences of their mental illnesses, but they also face all kinds of discriminatory barriers to good care based solely on their age. These include a lack of qualified mental health professionals, placement in board-and-care facilities or group homes where supervision and clinical support may be limited or minimal, and reduced funding for mental health services, to mention a few. And when mental health services are not integrated with other health care treatments, older adults with mental illnesses most often receive poorer quality mental health and medical care.

This kind of discrimination reduces the quality of life and worsens health outcomes. It may also lead to abuse and neglect. Although many of these individuals have much to contribute to society, they are systematically marginalized and cut off from avenues that would allow them to do so.[23]

Millions of Americans in their seventies, eighties, and nineties suffer from untreated depression and other mental illnesses. These are people whom we have failed. We can identify and effectively treat their common disorders, yet we lack the will to act upon what we know. We must reach out to these people wherever they are—isolated at home or in nursing homes or assisted living facilities. For so many, if given proper care, their final years can indeed be golden ones.

5.

WHEN DISASTER STRIKES

ONE DAY MANY, MANY years ago in Plains, I was taking the babysitter home. We had a station wagon back then, and Carrie Lee, the babysitter, was in the backseat with the baby, Jeff, who was about two at the time. This was long before seat belts even existed. All of a sudden I heard a loud crash and found myself frantically trying to hold onto the back of my seat as the car turned over in the air. I remember Carrie Lee screaming as she, too, scrambled to grab onto something. Someone had struck our car from the rear. It flipped completely over and landed sitting upright, facing in the opposite direction. Carrie Lee was not hurt, but she was still screaming. I didn't hear the baby at all. It was one of the worst moments of my life. Fortunately Jeff had been held in place by the spare tire. It had come out of the floor in the back part of the vehicle and kept him safe. He thought it was fun.

Someone took me to our business office in town, where

Jimmy was meeting with a customer. "I just totaled the car," I said in a trembling voice. I was shaking all over. He just said, "Where is it?" I told him, and on the way to get it, he dropped me off at home. He took care of everything, and I never saw the car again.

It was a miracle that no one was hurt. Carrie Lee had a tiny scratch just above her ankle that was not even deep enough to bleed, but I think we were both affected by the accident. I knew nothing about the psychological problems trauma can cause or about post-traumatic stress disorder (PTSD) back then, but for months afterward, I would begin to shake every time I picked up a newspaper. There were always reports of traffic accidents. I don't think I had noticed before that people could die just by running off the road into a ditch. After my own terrifying experience, whenever I saw the headline of an article about an accident, my heart raced. I became sweaty and shook all over, and it was a very long time before I could make myself drive past the place where my accident occurred.

Fortunately, Carrie Lee, Jeff, and I suffered no long-term or permanent consequences. We were so lucky. Since then I have been no stranger to trauma and catastrophic events. Through our work at The Carter Center over the past twenty-five years, Jimmy and I have traveled to more than sixty-five countries, and in too many instances, we have witnessed the devastating impacts of war and violence on innocent victims. I shall never forget the day in 1995 when we visited a refugee camp in the Sudan. Thousands of people were huddled in masses on the ground, sitting or lying down, waiting for help.

At a distance we could see a patch of blue—a makeshift tent made from a large sheet of plastic supported by sticks. It served as a health clinic for people who had come from far and near. A civil war had been raging in the country, and this was the first time in thirteen years that these people had had any health care at all.

As we stood looking at the site, we were overcome by the magnitude of the suffering. After taking a moment or two to regain our composure, we began walking through the masses in the direction of the blue tent. People were weak and sick, hollow eyed from hunger, staring into space, some shedding tears and others moaning. There was an occasional whimper from a child, but mostly it was eerily quiet, as though the people had no strength left with which to cry out. One little boy sobbed softly to me, "Mina, mina, mina." He was trying to tell me that he had stepped on a land mine. He had only one leg. My heart skipped a beat.

Seeing the children was the hardest for me.

As Jimmy and I walked among the people, we held babies and cuddled other small children, many with distended stomachs—a sign of starvation. I picked up one infant whose little arms fell limp at her sides. She was too weak to lift them. The doctor told me that she had malaria and would not live through the day. I could tell by the look in her mother's eyes that she already knew.

When we left the area, we were drained both physically and emotionally by the heat and the suffering and the shocking evidence of severe trauma that we had witnessed.

As I reflect on the anguish we saw that day, it gives me a renewed sense of urgency about the importance of providing help and support to victims of trauma—both children and adults. Its impact is so pervasive in our world, where violence, physical and mental abuse, poverty, natural disasters, and war continue to inflict pain on people of all ages.

What Is Trauma?

Each of us throughout our lifetime will experience traumatic events. It might be a discrete occurrence, like a car accident, a mugging, a fire, or a medical emergency that affects us personally. Trauma can also be a continuing presence in one's life. Child abuse, domestic violence, chronic illness—all can have persistent and harmful impacts. Train wrecks, plane crashes, bombings, floods, tornados, and earthquakes can be emotionally devastating. Disaster and catastrophe have been a part of the human condition forever. It is only recently, however, that we have begun to understand the significant mental health consequences of exposure to trauma.

Fortunately, most people who are exposed to terrifying ordeals do recover and go on with their lives. They may, like me after the car accident, experience symptoms of anxiety for some period of time, but eventually these subside and there are no lasting effects. For reasons we do not fully comprehend, others are not so fortunate.

We have learned much in the last twenty-five years about the effects of trauma on children, victims of natural disasters, and casualties of war, both military and civilian. We have begun to identify the factors that can influence how individuals respond to stress and whether or not they experience PTSD. Equally important, in the past decade both public officials and leaders in numerous disaster-relief organizations have made significant progress in developing more effective emergency response procedures. Yet despite these gains, it seems to me that we are losing ground in our fight to overcome the devastating consequences of trauma.

The Impact of PTSD

For some who are involved in a catastrophe or traumatic event, as well as some who witness it, healing can be elusive. PTSD affects about 3.5 percent of American adults[1] and can occur at any age, including in children. For millions, it can be accompanied by serious psychological problems: depression, substance abuse, or other anxiety disorders. Failure in school, criminal behavior, and even suicide can also result. There is some evidence that susceptibility to PTSD may run in families or is otherwise mediated by genetics. New research into what's happening at the genetic and brain-structure levels may hold some answers. In fact, unrecognized PTSD is common and can be an important contributor to severe depression.[2]

People with PTSD may startle easily and in an exaggerated way and become emotionally numb and withdrawn or extremely vigilant about potential danger. Depending on the severity of the trauma, they may lose interest in activities they usually enjoy; have trouble feeling affectionate; experience panic; be irritable; or engage in angry, aggressive, or violent outbursts. They may avoid situations that remind them of the original trauma, or they may become obsessed with them. If they become depressed, they can also experience all of the symptoms attendant with that disorder. Most people with PTSD have flashbacks, and they can also have nightmares.[3]

PTSD can develop after a terrifying ordeal that involves physical harm or the threat of physical harm to oneself, a loved one, or even a stranger. Natural and man-made disasters and a variety of random, more personal events such as robbery or rape can trigger it. In fact, PTSD seems to be worse if the harm was deliberately inflicted by another person rather than resulting from some natural disaster. When you think about it, it is easy to understand. Most of us have a harder time digesting that another person may have wanted to harm us or has no regard for us. This can undermine our faith in humanity and leave us feeling suspicious and isolated. In addition, a natural disaster is often experienced within a community, leaving many people struggling with the same issues at the same time. In such situations, the residents of the community support one another with a "we're all in this together" mentality. The aftermath of sexual assault, on the other hand, is often suffered in silence and alone, with victims possibly feeling stigmatized or mistakenly believing that they are somehow to blame for the crime perpetrated against them.

PTSD may emerge shortly after exposure to a traumatic event, or it may take months or even years before symptoms are obvious and a diagnosis is possible. No matter when it arises, for the afflicted and their families, the consequences are often devastating.

Protecting Our Children

Eleven-year-old Scott had been a B student, but his grades had dropped precipitously to Ds. When he came to see my friend Carl Bell, MD, and was asked about the reason for the sudden change, Scott said he just didn't know. After beginning therapy, the boy revealed that his father, who used to help him with his homework, had been shot to death in front of him in an elevator. The two were bystanders at an argument that turned violent. As the elevator climbed six stories, the boy helplessly witnessed his father dying from a wound to the abdomen. It was a gruesome scene, and the child vomited. Now, whenever he tried to study, he became nauseated.[4] This is a graphic example of the disastrous consequences of trauma on a child's mental well-being. The hopeful news is that with proper help, the boy was able to come to terms with the terrible event, overcome his nauseous response, and regain his successful study habits.

A growing body of evidence suggests that children exposed to traumatic events in early childhood can develop significant problems in later life, including substance abuse, obesity, depression, anxiety, and other serious conditions. Paul Fink, MD, a professor at Temple University and longtime advisor to my mental health program, has been studying this problem among at-risk children in Philadelphia, and he believes passionately that understanding the role trauma plays in the development of both physical and mental illnesses is going to revolutionize psychiatry forever.

Dr. Fink's concerns have been substantiated by research carried out by Vincent Felitti, MD, at Kaiser Permanente in California and his colleague Robert Anda, MD, at the Centers for Disease Control and Prevention. They analyzed the records of more than 18,000 Americans in order to understand the influence of what they called "adverse childhood experiences."[5] They discovered that some of the more intractable public health problems, like obesity, can have their roots in traumatic events that occurred many years before. "Time does not heal some of the adverse experiences of childhood," Dr. Felitti explained in an address he gave at The Carter Center for our symposium on the prevention of mental illnesses. "We came to recognize that the earliest years of infancy and childhood are not lost, but, like a child's footprints in wet cement, are often lifelong."[6]

The story of one of his patients, a young woman named Patty, clearly illustrates this link. Patty was enrolled in a weight-loss program run by Dr. Felitti. Initially dramatically overweight, in just one year she lost more than 130 pounds. But her success was short-lived. She soon began to put on weight again and within only a few months had regained every pound she had lost. In trying to understand what had happened, Dr. Felitti asked her why she thought this had occurred. "Actually, there is an older man at work," Patty finally admitted, "and he said, 'Hey, Patty, you're looking pretty good now. How about if we get together.'" In therapy,

Patty eventually revealed that she had repeatedly been sexually abused by her grandfather as a young girl and that finding herself sexualized by an older man had triggered a defense mechanism that she'd relied on when she was younger: She sought solace in food. Her trauma, like that of so many children, was hidden by time, shame, secrecy, and social taboos as she grew to adulthood, but the devastating impact was deep seated and long lasting.

Dr. Felitti's study concluded that there are nine categories of adverse childhood experiences, including recurrent physical abuse, substance abuse in the home, and an incarcerated family member. The greater the number of these experiences a person is exposed to, the worse the outcome in adulthood. For example, those who had had experiences in four or more of the categories were at much higher risk for drug abuse, alcoholism, and depression among other serious problems.

Untreated and unrecognized or hidden childhood traumas are one of our nation's most basic public health problems, underlying many of the rest of our societal scourges. These traumas can set in motion a whole host of risky behaviors that can eventually lead to social problems, incarceration, disease, disability, and even death. As Dr. Felitti explained at our symposium, "The costs of adverse childhood experiences are monumental, whether measured in dollars or the currency of humanity."[7] An important resource for mental health professionals, family members, educators, and others interested in child trauma is the National Child Traumatic Stress Network. This nationwide program, codirected by Robert Pynoos, MD, of UCLA, and John Fairbank, PhD, of Duke, provides educational materials, technical assistance, and other services throughout the country.

Lessons from Katrina

People struggling with mental illnesses and substance abuse may be more likely to have problems after a traumatic event when the fabric of the community is torn or destroyed. Hurricane Katrina traumatized a whole city and nation, but it was particularly injurious to people who were already living with a mental illness. As the entire infrastructure of New Orleans collapsed, 65 percent of the public mental health system disappeared with it: Twenty community mental health center outpatient offices were destroyed. A state psychiatric hospital filled to capacity with patients was rendered inoperable, and three of the four emergency inpatient psychiatric units were also ruined.[8] Medical records vanished, and people who were using medications suddenly lost their supplies, were unable to get more, and were left to roam the streets in aggravated states of withdrawal.

When the hurricane hit, James Cooper was office coordinator for the Extra Mile, an organization that links community and state agencies to meet the special needs of people with mental illnesses, developmental disabilities, or substance abuse problems. Cooper, in recovery from bipolar disorder and alcoholism, had lost two sons and his wife in an accident caused by a drunk driver just the year before. During the hurricane, he lost everything he owned, including his home.

At a November 2006 symposium at The Carter Center on disaster mental health in the wake of Hurricane Katrina, he described the nightmare in New Orleans.

> There was no way of communicating, of getting in touch with doctors or professionals to help, of being able to get out of the area. Cell phones and regular phones would not work. We were stuck there. Finally, after about the third day, they did bring ice and water. We had about ninety-five-degree temperatures, and trying to live in that heat without water, ice, electricity, and communications was terrible.

Mr. Cooper described how many people with mental illnesses were victimized during those early days. Then he concluded by saying that a year and a half after the disaster, there were still almost no services available and that many clients had turned to drugs or became suicidal because programs had not been restored.[9] The impact of the trauma endured long after the initial catastrophe.

Jeff Wellborn is the assistant commander of the New Orleans Police Department's Crisis Transportation Service. He helps those with mental health issues who come into contact with law enforcement, trying to keep them out of jail and securing appropriate services for them. During the hurricane, he was stationed at an operations center. "We had never seen it like this before," he told us at the symposium. "[The water] kept rising, and rising, and rising. Operations were down.

There were no telephones, lights, or plumbing." Worse for the police department was that communications failed when the Doppler radar was knocked out.

"We did not know what to do, and we are the guys who are supposed to have the answers," Wellborn said. "We are always supposed to know how to resolve situations, but when, all of a sudden, your communications are gone and your lights are out, it's a whole different story. Everybody starts getting nervous."[10]

The victims of Hurricane Katrina were not just those with serious mental illnesses or the elderly, mothers, and small children crammed into the New Orleans convention center. The first responders—the police, fire, and rescue personnel—were also affected by the events of the storm. Jeff talked about the "image armor" that accompanies a job in law enforcement. This is the notion that no tragedy, regardless of how horrific, can traumatize police because they are invincible, they have seen everything. But we know this is not the case. First responders are not immune to fear and anxiety. They can also suffer from compassion fatigue and burnout, which may lead them to respond inappropriately in difficult situations and to develop serious mental health problems later on.

Lessons must be learned from this tragedy. We must make sure that mental health is a priority in the planning, preparedness, and response policies put in place for potential future disasters. We need regional reciprocity for licensed professionals during a disaster, which would allow a clinical psychologist or social worker licensed to work in Georgia, for example, to go to Louisiana to help without having to get a license there. We need to computerize medical records so they are easily accessible when clinics or doctors' offices are destroyed. We need to include psychiatric drugs in emergency stockpiles of medications. And, we must pay attention to the mental health needs of first responders as well as of victims. Most importantly, we must do a much better job of organizing for disaster response in the first place.

The Importance of Leadership in the Face of Crisis

Disasters—both natural and man-made—are part of our history, and throughout this history both government and the private sector have had important roles to play in alleviating their traumatic effects.

Today federal and state governments are crucial participants in disaster response and can have a dramatic impact on the psychological reactions of people in distress. When Jimmy was president, he recognized that multiple agencies spread across numerous departments provided services to state and local governments during times of disaster and that this often produced uncoordinated, unwieldy, and ineffective results. In 1979 he signed an executive order that brought all of these services under the umbrella of the Federal Emergency Management Agency (FEMA), whose director reported directly to the White House. The consolidation brought much better coordination and efficiency to relief efforts, ensuring that the needs of the people afflicted by a major disaster could be clearly communicated to the president without having to go through layers of bureaucracy. Since then, FEMA has responded to more than 2,800 presidentially declared disasters.

Unfortunately, in 2003, FEMA was folded into the Department of Homeland Security. This meant that the agency no longer had a direct line to the president and once again was subject to a whole host of bureaucratic forces. Certainly, the reorganization contributed to the disastrous nonresponse to Hurricane Katrina, one of the government's largest system failures in our history.

The lack of coordination and leadership during and after the hurricane has had devastating consequences for hundreds of thousands of people in New Orleans and the other affected areas nearby. Yet we know how to do better. In the aftermath of the storm, the director of my mental health program at The Carter Center, Thom Bornemann, EdD, led a team trained in disaster relief to Houston to help the Mental Health and Mental Retardation Authority of Harris County. In that one city, the mental health needs of both its citizens and two hundred and forty thousand Katrina evacuees were met because state and local officials worked together, effectively led by Mayor Bill White. Each morning the leaders from all disaster response sectors gathered to assess their progress toward improving service delivery. The focus was on getting the right resources deployed most effectively against the most urgent and serious problems. In the days just after the disaster, the teams in Houston were able to provide residents and evacuees with the critical elements that are so important for reducing psychological distress, such as housing, income support, and school for the children.

Leadership in the face of a major traumatic event is vital to the success of the overall response. This was demonstrated so clearly in the days and months after the 9/11 terrorist attacks with Mayor Rudy Giuliani's response in New York City. His actions demonstrated how powerful a steady hand and skilled communication can be in the face of very dark hours. Mayor Giuliani kept the general public informed about immediate steps being taken by the city, state, and federal governments and communicated a sense of shared grief. He balanced the need to move forward while still acknowledging the pain and fear surrounding the tragic loss of so many loved ones. During a traumatic event, strong leadership helps people and communities maintain a sense of structure and safety.

The Plight of Our Veterans— A National Disgrace

We know that when someone has increased and prolonged exposure to traumatic events or circumstances, that person is more likely to have psychological distress and PTSD. As I write this, more than 1.8 million US troops have been sent to fight in Afghanistan and Iraq. It is estimated that between 14 and 18 percent of these returning vets have PTSD and another 14 percent have major depression.[11] This means that at least 300,000 of our young men and women are struggling with the emotional aftereffects of their wartime experiences. But these numbers, as high as they are, may underestimate the true scope of this problem. Tours of duty in combat areas are getting longer, redeployment is common, and breaks between tours are infrequent and too short. Indeed, the US Army's fifth Mental Health Advisory Team (MHAT-V) surveyed about 3,000 soldiers in Iraq and Afghanistan and reported that while the rate of mental health problems for veterans returning from their first deployment is approximately 18 percent, more than a quarter of those soldiers serving a third tour of duty have a disorder.[12]

But this doesn't mean that they receive help. For instance, soldiers returning from Iraq fill out questionnaires that are supposed to warn officials if they are at risk for depression, PTSD, or alcohol or drug use. Yet a study by the investigative arm of Congress, the Government Accountability Office, suggests a national trend: About 80 percent of the soldiers who showed potential signs of PTSD were not referred for mental health care.[13]

Lance Corporal Patrick Uloth had served two deployments as a Marine in Iraq and was awarded a medal for his bravery in the battle at Fallujah. During his second tour, Uloth witnessed a suicide bombing in which one of his platoonmates was blown up. The same explosion also killed a close friend. When he returned to Camp Pendleton in California, he began behaving erratically. He went days without sleeping. Formerly gentle with his wife, he shoved her against a wall and became aggressive with her. He experienced uncontrollable trembling and memory loss—all symptoms of PTSD.

After he suffered seizures and hallucinations, he went to the mental health center at the base seeking help, only to be told that he would have to wait for three to six months before he could be seen.

Unable to get adequate treatment at Camp Pendleton, he checked into a psychiatric facility at an Air Force base in Mississippi. There, he was arrested for going AWOL, taken away in chains, jailed for two months, given a "less than honorable" discharge, and denied any further medical or military benefits—despite his diagnosis of PTSD. Uloth's plight was brought to the nation's attention by National Public Radio reporter Daniel Zwerdling,[14] who came to The Carter Center to talk with our mental health journalism fellows about this most shameful national dilemma.

Zwerdling also told us about Tyler Jennings, who had returned from Iraq to Fort Carson in Colorado.[15] He was so depressed and desperate that he turned to the medical center at his base for help. His records indicate that he suffered from "crying spells . . . hopelessness . . . helplessness . . . worthlessness"—typical signs of PTSD and depression. He, too, was turned away. When he couldn't get the help he needed, he tried drugs.

Jennings told Zwerdling that when the sergeants who ran his platoon discovered he was having a breakdown and taking drugs, they started to haze him. No one was allowed to interact with him—he was made to sit in a corner like a "dunce," and they threatened to expel him from the army. As a result, he began planning a suicide attempt and almost went through with it. Another serviceman, Jason Harvey, slashed his wrists and arms in a cry for help. Officials at Fort Carson expelled Harvey from the army for "patterns of misconduct." Harvey, too, had been diagnosed with PTSD.

The wars in Iraq and Afghanistan have also placed women in high-profile combat positions that have exposed them to the risk of injury and death. But very little is being discussed about their specific issues, particularly if they are suffering from PTSD and return to primary caregiver roles.

Given these many issues, the MHAT-V found that 15 to 20 percent of married service members deployed for longer than a year were considering divorce or separation. Military families experience tremendous stress in association with multiple, long-term tours of duty coupled with the medical and psychiatric problems that returning veterans carry home with them.[16] Added to that are changes in family roles that occur during the service members' deployments. Spouses left behind often become the family's sole decision makers, and then there is an adjustment period when the military partner returns. It is no wonder that many marriages do not survive this period.

Family disruptions are of great concern to military health officials because divorce is the greatest risk factor for suicide among our service members.[17] And, quite alarmingly, these suicides are on the rise. The number reported by the US Army has risen to the highest level since record keeping began three decades ago. In the six years since the war in Iraq began, the rate among active-duty and inactive reserve-status soldiers has doubled. In addition to failed relationships, legal and financial problems and job stress were found to contribute to these deaths. There was also a significant connection between suicide attempts and the number of days served.[18] Evidence suggests that the psychological toll from these deployments is even more devastating than the physical injuries of combat.[19]

The military is working to correct these difficulties, but staffing problems and burnout are a hindrance. When the MHAT-V team surveyed 131 mental health professionals in the war zones, they reported being short of personnel and equipment. Their own mental health was at risk, as well, and their performance was hampered by their own long deployments. In 2008, the Army was trying to hire 275 more mental health professionals to work in the United States and Europe, but had only found 148.[20] I am hopeful that the very recent initiatives put in place by the army to address these critical problems will bring about much needed improvements.

How can we ask our young men and women to serve and protect us and then ignore them when they are most in need? We support our troops in the field, but it is critical that we continue to support them when they come home. Their physical injuries—lost limbs, brain injuries, bullet wounds—may be obvious to us, but emotional damage, even if the body is whole, is harder to detect. That doesn't make those injuries any less important. Finally, we cannot ignore the countless thousands of National Guard and reserve troops who have also experienced long deployments in the war zones. They face even greater challenges, for they are likely to have even fewer treatment services available to them than members of the regular armed forces do upon their return to civilian life. We may need to think about unconventional ways to reach out to employers to clarify with them the issues that returning vets face in the workplace. Since many psychological and substance abuse issues only come to light well after these troops are deactivated, how do we provide adequate, timely, and appropriate services for these heroes?

Jeannie Ritter, wife of Colorado governor Bill Ritter, has started an innovative new program to help returning veterans in her own state. In cooperation with local mental health advocates, foundations, and corporations, Jeannie leads a program that connects local citizens with returning troops to offer support. The troops and their families are also informed about services that are available from their local community mental health centers so they know where to go if they are experiencing mental or emotional problems. This is the kind of effort we need in every state in our country.

The Need for Much Greater Investment

There is so much we can do at the government, community, care-provider, and individual levels to ensure that when a traumatic event occurs, strong leadership and supports and services will be in place to respond to the crisis. Providing help and support to the victims of trauma—both children and adults—is very important in preventing future emotional problems.

One of the most intriguing approaches that I have learned about is the concept of psychological first aid. It was created to help children, adolescents, adults, and families in the immediate aftermath of disasters and terrorist attacks and is designed to reduce the initial psychological distress caused by traumatic events. It provides tools and techniques to promote a sense of safety, calm, empowerment, and hope.[21]

How does it work? Let's say a preschooler sees a car accident. His response may be to stop talking and just stare. The recommended psychological first aid would be to help this child express his fears by playacting, drawing, or talking about it. Or what if a teenager has witnessed violence in her community? Post-traumatic responses such as drug use, delinquency, or inappropriate sexual behavior can be lessened if she can understand that her behavior is an effort to numb the pain. It might also help her to voice her anger about the event.

While psychological first aid is growing in influence and importance, we need more research on effective treatments, for there is much more to be done. We need a global approach to the problem of trauma and PTSD. The President's New Freedom Commission on Mental Health recommended that the National Institutes of Health undertake a sustained program of research on the impact of trauma on the mental health of specific populations: women, children, and the victims of violent crime, including terrorism. The return of our veterans from Iraq and Afghanistan has brought a renewed interest in research on the treatment of PTSD and traumatic brain injury, and on suicide prevention. The attention these issues are receiving has also encouraged further investigation into their impact on families. I would go further and say that we should increase our research efforts to better understand these conditions and their treatment over the long term. We must do more.

6.

DOING TIME FOR A MENTAL ILLNESS

WHEN I WAS A little girl in Plains, I occasionally encountered a young man who would wander up and down the street nervously. He wasn't around all the time, but when he appeared, he frightened me, and I always ran and hid from him. When I grew older, I learned that he was Jimmy's cousin Linton, and when he disappeared from town, he was at Central State Hospital, the large state mental institution in Milledgeville, Georgia. I didn't know then what his diagnosis was, but despite his mother's efforts to care for him, he was not always able to live at home.

Every so often he would get very loud on the street and everyone would know he was in trouble again. Soon the sheriff would pick him up, give him a shot, sometimes even put him in a straitjacket, and take him back to the hospital.

Linton's condition—and the way he was treated—made a great impression on me as a child. I hadn't thought about him for many years, however, until one evening at The Carter Center when we organized a special screening of Joseph Greco's semiautobiographical *Canvas,* a remarkable film that tells the story of a family in Florida struggling to deal with the mother's serious mental illness.

One scene reminded me of my childhood experiences with Linton. Mary, the mother, is slipping into the terrible grip of schizophrenia and runs outside in her nightgown in the middle of a raging thunderstorm. As her husband, John, tries desperately to bring her back inside, she becomes more and more agitated. Alarmed neighbors call the police. While her ten-year-old son Chris watches in horror, the police overpower her, handcuff her, and force her into the backseat of a squad car—just like Jimmy's cousin. The look of terror and confusion on her face says more than words ever could about how wrong it is to treat people with mental illnesses as though they are criminals.

Sadly, we do this all too often. Indeed, it is a problem of staggering proportions. More than 15 percent of people in jails and prisons have a severe mental illness, and a recent report found that only one-fourth of those in federal prisons and only one-sixth of those in local jails received any kind of treatment.[1] An estimated 40 percent of people with a serious mental illness will come in contact with the criminal justice system at some time in their lives. We must no longer tolerate this inappropriate treatment's exorbitant costs to society or terrible consequences for these individuals.

Abuse and Neglect Come Full Circle

Two hundred and fifty years ago, when our nation lacked any system of care for indigent people with mental illnesses, they were often dropped off at local jails, where they were chained in cages, beaten, and otherwise abused. The situation remained relatively unchanged until the mid-1800s, when Massachusetts reformer Dorothea Dix started the movement to provide more humane treatment.

Initially the care provided in these new institutions was a great improvement over the horrifying treatment so many had suffered in jails and poorhouses. But over time these large public institutions began to deteriorate, and by the mid-1900s patients were once more living in the most deplorable conditions.

Then, enlightened leaders proposed a network of community mental health centers around the country that would allow people to get help close to home. If we had had those services when Linton was a young man, he might have been spared the trauma of his frequent trips in the police car to Central State Hospital.

While I was First Lady, I learned much more about this policy of deinstitutionalization—moving people out of hospitals and back to their own communities. Instead of being the answer to providing better care—for which we had such high hopes—it was a dismal failure because only about half of the local mental health centers were ever built. When I testified before the late Senator Ted Kennedy in 1979 about the findings of our President's Commission on Mental Health, I told him and the other committee members that the plight of Americans with chronic mental illnesses was clearly one of the most pressing problems we faced. I described how many were released from state hospitals and returned to their communities before any services were available, only to lead marginal existences on the fringes of society, jobless, homeless, and often hungry. They desperately needed comprehensive services—helping networks near home, family, and friends.[2]

During the next year, we developed a national plan to provide people with chronic mental illnesses with housing, employment, and good health and mental health care—the same basic needs we all share—all in their own communities. The plan also included far-reaching recommendations about financing these reforms, but it was never implemented.

Hundreds of thousands of individuals were released from state hospitals, but the alternatives they faced were just as awful. Many of them became the men and women who now inhabit abandoned buildings or sleep on park benches and spend their days on street corners asking for spare change. Many more turned to alcohol or drug use to help ease their pain. Some ran afoul of the law, but for many others jails and prisons were simply the providers of last resort when our mental health system failed to offer them the appropriate care. Tragically, the situation is only getting worse today.

Jails and Prisons—
Our New "System" of Care

Fifty years ago there were more than a half-million people in public psychiatric hospitals around the country. Today there are slightly more than fifty thousand—a reduction of 90 percent.[3] This does not mean that we have accomplished the goal of enabling people to live successfully in their own communities. Instead, we have simply moved many of them to our prisons and jails. In the Los Angeles County Jail, for example, there are 1,400 people with serious mental health and substance use problems, making it the largest mental health facility in the country.[4]

Jails and prisons can be terrifying for anyone, but for people with severe mental illnesses, this is especially true. Many correctional facilities do not have qualified mental health professionals on their staffs to recognize and respond to the needs of inmates experiencing severe psychiatric symptoms. In some instances, doctors whose licenses have been revoked practice in correctional institutions, in many cases giving substandard, criminally neglectful care.[5] Prison officials frequently react to psychotic inmates by punishing them or placing them in physical restraints or in isolation. But these responses can worsen rather than alleviate symptoms. Often, access to medications is limited due to cost constraints, and rarely are rehabilitative services available that could help a discharged prisoner transition successfully into the community.

In 2006, Michele Gillen, the chief investigative reporter for television station WFOR in Miami, produced a shocking exposé of the horrific conditions on the ninth floor of the Miami-Dade Detention Center, which was overflowing with people diagnosed with mental illnesses. Virtually abandoned on what was called the "Forgotten Floor," these men were crammed three and four to a cell meant to hold a single inmate. Many cells did not have clean running water. Each cell had a single steel shelf that the prisoners took turns sleeping on while their cellmates slept on the filthy floor or under the shelf. All were accused but not convicted of crimes, and most were arrested for minor infractions for which the average person would have been set free in a matter of hours. Yet, they were locked into the crowded cells for days, weeks, or months and allowed out for only fifteen minutes twice a week.[6]

After a lawsuit was filed to protect the rights of these individuals, Miami-Dade County judge Steven Leifman was appointed special advisor on criminal justice and mental health to advise the Supreme Court of Florida on how to correct this situation. "We never deinstitutionalized," he concluded. "What we in fact did was trans-institutionalized. We transferred people from really horrible state hospitals to really horrible jails. But we also gave them criminal records, making it more difficult for them to go into recovery. With a criminal record it is harder to find employment and housing."[7] In Florida at this point, there were five times as many people with mental illnesses in jails as there were in psychiatric hospitals.[8] As the chief psychiatrist at the Miami-Dade Detention Center, Joseph Poitier, MD, concluded sadly, "We are reverting to how it was in the sixteenth and seventeenth centuries. This is morally incomprehensible."[9] We have indeed come full circle—with very tragic consequences.

Who Are These "Criminals"?

For many years I have been involved with Project Interconnections (PI), a program in Atlanta that provides housing and other services for people with serious mental illnesses. Diane White, a resident of O'Hern House, one of four sites PI operates in the city, told me that when she was about twelve years old, she began to realize that something was amiss. When she was in her early twenties she was diagnosed with serious depression, but she could tell by her mood swings and the way her character changed from day to day that something else was wrong. Subsequently, she was diagnosed with bipolar disorder.

One day she was walking through a section of town where narcotics were bought and sold when police arrived, handcuffed her, and told her they knew she had just purchased drugs. She denied their allegations and said she was not guilty. But there was drug paraphernalia all around, and they insisted that some of it belonged to her. They shoved her into a squad car, took her to the police station, and put her in jail. There she stayed for five months without any medication or access to legal assistance. Finally, a public defender came to see her. At first he wanted her to sign a document admitting her guilt, but she steadfastly refused. "No way [would I do it]," she told me. "It'll stay with you all your life that you were guilty of narcotics . . . and I wasn't." Finally, the lawyer asked her to write down exactly what had happened the day the police picked her up. She carefully described all that had taken place, and by the end of the day the public defender had obtained her release.[10]

Sadly, there were no services provided to help Diane successfully transition back into the community or manage her illness. She started to medicate herself—first with alcohol, then with marijuana and finally cocaine. She abandoned her children, ended up homeless, and lived on the streets for fourteen years.

Without access to good mental health care and other supportive services, individuals like Diane often end up struggling to survive and are put at greatly increased risk for running afoul of our law enforcement system. When they do get into trouble, it makes their mental health issues even worse. The failure to create good community-based mental health services across our country means that people like Diane have nowhere to turn. Substance use problems typically add further complexity to their situations—either initially or over time. An estimated 80 percent of all people with mental illnesses in our jails and prisons have dual diagnoses—which means that along with the mental disorder, they also struggle with substance use.[11] These individuals typically have more serious health and social problems, need more costly care, including hospitalization, and are at higher risk for homelessness.

Most of these people do not belong in prison. They are not dangerous to themselves or others. They end up incarcerated because, like Diane, they were in the "wrong place at the wrong time" or they have committed a nonviolent crime. Trespassing, having an open container of alcohol, shoplifting, disturbing the peace—these are violations of the law, but they should not condemn a person to weeks, months, or even years of abuse and neglect in prison. This distresses me greatly, for it need not happen at all.

For those who are impoverished or have become so because of their mental illnesses, help is especially hard to come by—and often they can't get any help at all until they are in an acute psychotic state, at which point they may well be dangerous to themselves or to others. So once again, our jails and prisons become the treatment centers of last resort. We know this is wrong. My friend and colleague Kathryn Power, director of the Center for Mental Health Services, summarized the problem well: "Justice facilities never were intended to be mental health treatment centers. The aims and conditions of incarceration actually work *against* recovery. . . . Incarceration takes from individuals any control over their own lives, making them feel powerless and vulnerable. Punishment will not 'cure' a mental illness—but it can make it worse."[12]

Even more distressing is that for some people with mental illnesses, incarceration leads to further victimization and unspeakable kinds of abuse. Nora Haynes is the former president of the National Alliance on Mental Illness (NAMI) Georgia affiliate. Her son, Joey, has struggled with schizophrenia for many years. At one point Joey ended up in federal custody but was housed in a local Georgia jail. "He was put in a cell with a lot of violent offenders," says Nora, "and they destroyed him. He had to go to the emergency room. It was just a nightmare." Eventually, he was so badly hurt that jail officials placed him in solitary confinement. But as Nora said, "The last thing a person with mental illness needs is to be isolated in a cell."

Another group—a very small minority—also deserves our care and attention: individuals with serious mental illnesses who have in fact committed and been convicted of serious crimes. Although a majority of the American public still believes that people with mental illnesses are violent, only 26 percent of people with mental illnesses in our prisons are incarcerated for violent offenses.[13] Our obligation to them is to ensure their safety and provide for their health and mental health care needs. Today, in many prisons we fail on both fronts.

How Do We Help People Like Diane?

One hundred years ago, Diane White might have been sent to a state mental institution. Instead, the Atlanta city jail became her treatment center. Of course, like state institutions a century ago, most jails do very little that promotes recovery, and the experience certainly did not help her. For those who finally are released, like Diane, recovery can remain elusive for many years as they struggle to simply survive—often on the streets.

As many as three-quarters of a million people are homeless every day in our country,[14] and California has the largest homeless population. The City of San Francisco estimates that

70 percent of its homeless have a mental illness or are substance users—or both. Throughout the state, about 50,000 mentally ill people sleep on the street each night.[15] Behind these staggering numbers are real individuals like Diane.

So what can and should we be doing to correct this terrible situation? The answers seem so simple. We need to keep people with mental illnesses out of jail in the first place. If they are incarcerated, they need proper mental health and rehabilitative services and help transitioning back into their own communities. Once in their own communities, they may need several different kinds of assistance to move toward recovery and have opportunities to participate fully in community life. We know what to do. We have studied this problem for decades. We have even implemented some good solutions on a very small scale that could be replicated across the country. We need the political will to make it happen.

Keeping the "Criminals" Out of Jail: Diversion Programs

There are a variety of diversion programs that have proven effective in keeping people out of jails and prisons by redirecting individuals with serious mental illnesses from jail to community-based treatment and support services. Over the past two decades, these programs have emerged as a viable and humane solution to inappropriate criminal detention.

Today there are more than three hundred jail diversion programs operating nationally. There are two types. Prebooking programs divert individuals when they initially come into contact with law enforcement officers, before formal charges are brought. Postbooking programs divert them at some point after arrest and booking and are either court or jail based.[16]

On a cool October morning I drove to Albany, Georgia, thirty-five miles from Plains, to see firsthand how a prebooking diversion program works. As I stepped into a courtroom at the county courthouse, I saw several people chatting. It was a small, intimate room, not like the large, forbidding ones I remembered—although I must admit that I have been in only one or two courtrooms in my entire life. Judge Steve Goss recognized and welcomed me. Then he introduced me to his staff, which included a registered nurse, a caseworker for mental health and another for substance use, one district attorney, one assistant public defender, and three probation officers.

This morning, Judge Goss explained, he was conducting a mental health court. As a state trial judge with felony jurisdiction, he kept seeing the same defendants with obvious mental health problems over and over again. They would typically appear with a probation violation charge such as a drug test failure or a new misdemeanor charge, which would often coincide with some stressful event that had caused them to stop taking their medications or to begin to "self-medicate" with alcohol or street drugs. Their mental state would deteriorate and they would land back in jail. These cases clogged the docket, filling the jails with people who needed help, not punishment, and frustrating both law enforcement and judiciary staff, who knew they were not trained to provide what was needed. The mental health court provides a far better alternative for addressing their problems.

Judge Goss told me that he would be less formal than he is in regular court, but he went on to say that it was not his style to be too informal. In light of that, I was surprised and heartened by the warm and friendly way he greeted the first defendant. "Good morning, Claire," he said to a tall and attractive woman. "How are you doing today? You're looking mighty good."

"I'm doing okay," she said. "I brought my thirteen-year-old home. Got my three boys home now. I am working full-time. . . . Just had my vacation and spent it taking care of my grandmother, who had surgery."

Judge Goss turned to her probation officer and inquired about how Claire was doing. The answer: "She's doing good on probation. Going to central AA twice a week, has worked for one year, is keeping in contact with me." It was a very positive report. Judge Goss looked at Claire and said, "I understand you are doing well considering your domestic problems. I want to get you off probation. Come back next month. If you have a good report—you're staying in touch with your caseworker, drug free, and taking your medicine— we can look to the termination of care successfully on our next date. Good luck. Have a nice weekend." Everyone in the room was pleased with Claire's progress toward recovery, and she left with a big smile on her face.

As the defendants came into the courtroom one at a time, the judge and his staff appeared genuinely glad to see each one of them. They congratulated those who were making good progress and offered support and second chances to those who were not. Sophie, a middle-aged woman who was well known to the court team, had been picked up the prior afternoon and brought to the jail, where she had spent the night. Sophie suffered from delusions and sometimes thought she was a prophet. She had been imprisoned originally because she had tried to "lay hands on" someone who had objected. The mental health court team had been working with her to get her stabilized and had found a place in a local church facility for her to stay. But the day before, she had left without warning and ended up in a bar. One of the team members had gone to get her, taken her to a pharmacy to get her medication, and then brought her back to the jail for the night.

This morning she was still agitated. The caseworker had tried to confirm that she had taken her medicine, but it was difficult to know. Pills were gone, but she might have simply thrown them away. Sophie quarreled with the deputy sheriff, Sergeant Rick Windham, who brought her into the room. "Get your hands off me," she shouted, "I am a woman of the cloth." After a further exchange, she looked at Judge Goss and said plaintively, "I want to tell you something."

"Okay," he replied, "just go ahead and tell us."

"Help me," she pleaded. It struck me that Sophie's was the voice of so many in our prisons today.

"I am going to help you . . . and you are going to be all right," Judge Goss gently assured her, and then he referred her to the prison doctor. Sergeant Windham was still holding her arm, and I heard him say quietly to her, "You know I love you. Now come with me," before he led her from the room.

Some of the police in Albany, including Sergeant Windham, have been specially trained to work with people with mental illnesses, and the training is ongoing. There is also a nurse who evaluates all prisoners. Those who are thought to have a mental illness are further evaluated to determine if they should go to the mental health court or be incarcerated. If a crime involves a firearm, a person is not eligible for the mental health program. But Judge Goss is a remarkably enlightened official. The next defendant to appear before him, a teenage boy, came in handcuffed.

"David is just somebody I wanted to come back today and check in with us," Judge Goss told me. "David has a mental illness and was continuously taunted at school. One day he got really mad [and] went and got a shotgun. It was wrestled out of his hands before anyone got hurt, but it did go off, and, of course, he was arrested and spent the night in jail."

When David was first evaluated, the doctor said he should not go to jail because his illness had caused him to "act out." Because a weapon was involved, he was not eligible for the court, but Judge Goss had assigned a caseworker to work with him and his family. She kept track of him and advised the judge when difficulties arose. Now he was having a problem with his medication and needed to see a doctor. "Yesterday wasn't soon enough," said Judge Goss. "This young man has always reported to the staff as instructed, but the real problem is getting a doctor's appointment for a person with a mental illness. His mother told the caseworker she had tried and tried, but that it would be over three months before anyone would see him."

He then turned to David. "The nurse will check with the doctor, and we'll get you an appointment next week. Take your medicine. We don't want to see you back in jail."

David left the courtroom and the judge explained to me, "We couldn't send that young man to prison. It would ruin his life. If we get a young person who has no history with the law [who] comes in and pleads guilty, he's not sentenced. He can be in the program for one year and if he behaves, the DA can preadjudicate and dismiss the case."

I stayed until the very last case was heard. After working in the mental health field for so long, it was a great experience for me to see people with mental illnesses being treated with such compassion and respect. I was overwhelmed. When I left the court, Sergeant Windham escorted me out, and as we walked along, I told him how impressed I was by all that I had seen and heard that morning. I said that I had even heard him say to Sophie that he loved her and how out of character that was for a policeman. He said, "Judge Goss teaches us how to work with the people who come to our court, and we have learned that it always makes a difference."

Crisis Intervention Teams:
Another Effective Solution

Since our law enforcement personnel are often on the front lines when it comes to identifying people with mental illnesses and directing them to the right resources, it's imperative that they know how to deal with someone who is in the middle of a mental health crisis. If not, tragedies can and do occur. Trish Solomon, who works for us at The Carter Center, told me about her uncle, Willie Luke Thurman Jr., who died in the custody of the Grand Rapids police department in Michigan at the age of fifty-two.

Willie had been diagnosed with paranoid schizophrenia, and for a large part of his life he was on medications to control it. They helped, but every ten years or so, he would have a relapse, which usually resulted in paranoia, delusions, and auditory hallucinations. In 2003, he had such an episode.

"He awoke early one morning," Trish explained, "and started his daily walk to his parents' home some five or six blocks away. It was his birthday. He saw an unmanned car running [to warm the engine], as is often the case on a crisp Michigan morning. In his delusional state, he thought it was a surprise birthday gift from his family, so he got in. He was arrested and taken to the county jail. During the booking process officers took his glasses, and he became agitated and then combative. The police sprayed him with pepper spray and left him until he fell unconscious. He was taken to the hospital, where he was pronounced brain-dead from a lack of oxygen to the brain. Some days later, he died."[17]

Tragedies like these can and must be avoided. Our police officers need to know how to deal with someone who is experiencing a mental health crisis. Fortunately, programs around the country are helping to train them in how to respond. Before I left the Albany court, Judge Goss had told me that he and his staff work closely with the local crisis intervention team (CIT).

I had learned about CITs at a Carter Center meeting when Georgia's program was just beginning. I sat at a table that night with police chief Sam Cochran of Memphis, Tennessee, who was largely responsible for creating the program, and his partner in the effort, Randy Dupont, PhD, a mental health professional, professor at the University of Memphis, and expert in crisis de-escalation. Sam told me how the CIT program first started. Back in the mid-1980s, there was a tragic episode in Memphis in which police officers answered a crisis call involving a young man with a serious mental illness who was cutting himself with a large knife. The incident ended with the young man being shot repeatedly. The Memphis community was outraged, and city officials realized they needed to act immediately to find a better way to respond to crisis events. A partnership was formed among the Memphis Police Department, NAMI, mental health providers, the University of Memphis, and the University of Tennessee, and the CIT program was developed. In a forty-hour training program, special squads of patrol officers are taught how to identify someone who is in crisis, how to de-escalate the situation, and where to divert the individuals instead of arresting them.[18]

Today Sam and Randy lead a national effort to develop these programs. The costs are minimal because training is provided free by mental health professionals and advocates—mostly members of NAMI—and the police also participate on a voluntary basis. The program clearly is making a difference. Memphis has seen a decrease in the rate of arrests of people in crisis, an impressive rate of diversion into the mental health care system, and a reduction in the number of people with mental illness in the jails.[19] And importantly, officer injury has decreased sevenfold.[20] These significant results are being replicated around the country. In Miami-Dade County, for instance, the CIT program has lowered arrest rates, as well as police injuries, and reduced police shootings drastically.[21]

In my own state, advocates led by Nora Haynes approached the Georgia Bureau of Investigation about bringing the CIT model here. Vernon Keenan, the bureau's director, enthusiastically embraced the idea and is now establishing CIT statewide. He was responsible for making sure that the program was incorporated on a broader scale through our state's Peace Officer Standards and Training Council. This has allowed a variety of law enforcement officers to participate, including those in university police departments, sheriff's departments, and other police departments. The Georgia program has been highly successful and received the International Association of Chiefs of Police Civil Rights Award in 2008. Keenan also has been cited for his efforts.

Recently I had the chance to talk with a young man who has been helped by this program. His story is both frightening and full of hope. Tyler Lee Barnett grew up an only child in northern Georgia. His father died before he was born, and since his mother had to work, he was raised mostly by his grandparents. Tyler is now in his twenties and has bipolar disorder. He told me that for years, he hung out with "the wrong group," drinking, smoking marijuana, getting into trouble, and giving his family a hard time.

One day shortly after his girlfriend left him, taking with her their baby girl, Tyler learned that one of his best friends had been killed. He got drunk and stayed drunk. "I couldn't stand reality," he said. "It hurt. I drew inward. I was mad all the time and frustrated because I had no idea what to do. I got into fights with my best friends and yelled at my mama and grandparents. I let down everyone I loved . . . and all this time I was trying not to let anyone see how much I was hurting. Reality was too much to deal with. I was going downhill fast."

Then at home he "went wild," raging through the house. Alarmed and frightened, his grandmother called 911. Tyler told her to tell the operator that he would "kill any cop" who came to take him away. Then he got his grandfather's machete and waited in the bathroom for the police to arrive. Soon— with sirens screaming—they did. Now alone in the house, Tyler described how he looked out a window, saw a cop behind a bush with his gun drawn, and knew that whatever happened next would not be good. The phone started to ring and kept on ringing. Eventually, Tyler picked it up. Much to his surprise, a man introduced himself as Captain James Scott and asked what he could do to help.

"I didn't want to help myself, but this man was actually willing to help me, and he was unarmed," Tyler said. "I put the machete down, and I told him to tell the other officers to lower their weapons and I would come outside. Much to my surprise, they did. I was still on edge but finally went to the screen door. Captain Scott was there and I asked, 'Haven't you ever had a bad day before?' 'Yes,' he replied, 'and you are going to be all right. Come with me and we will talk. Just me and you. Nobody is going to hurt you.' So we sat down on the tailgate of my Papa's truck and I began to explain to the captain as best I could what was going on."

Scott, a CIT-trained police officer, was able to peacefully resolve a potentially deadly situation and get Tyler to treatment. Even today Scott regularly checks on him and helps when his grandparents call occasionally because he is not taking his medication. The words of his grandmother moved me deeply: "We respect and are truly thankful for Captain Scott, CIT, and Judge Brown [Tyler's probation judge], all of whom understand how vulnerable and fragile a person with mental illness can be at times. It is my hope that through this program [CIT] many will come to a better understanding of the complexity of this illness. It is treatable. These ill people are deserving of our respect and understanding. We are extremely thankful that Tyler is a part of our family. We love him—always have—always will."

Addressing the Root Causes
of Criminalization: We Need to Act Now

Mental health courts and crisis intervention training can help keep people with serious mental illnesses from landing in jail, but these are at best only partial solutions to the problem of criminalization. Real progress will require fundamental changes in the mental health systems that have so tragically deviated from their goal of promoting community living with dignity.[22]

For far too long, opponents of comprehensive community-based services have argued that they are simply too expensive and we don't have enough money for them. But consider this: A recent study of the cost savings associated with a mental health court program in Pittsburgh found that the county saved more than $3.3 million over two years after implementing the new program for the Allegheny County jail system.[23] Imagine investing all that money in community-based services. Other studies have shown that investing in good mental health programs can save many multiples of the investment amount because criminal activity and hospitalizations are significantly reduced.[24]

At Project Interconnections, people like Diane White find the support they need to live successfully in the community. After fifteen years of homelessness complicated by continued drug use, Diane remembers the day in 2005 when her son called from New York, where he was living with his grandparents. "Do you remember what life was like before you were on drugs?" he asked. She couldn't remember. To mask her pain, she went on an eight-day binge. At the end of it, she entered a rehabilitation program at St. Jude's Recovery Center in Atlanta. While she was in treatment, she would often pass the building next door as she went out looking for work. There were always people gathered around the doorstep, smoking. One day she paused to talk with them and discovered they were clients of Community Friendship, a nonprofit psychiatric rehabilitation center in the city. She began to attend some of their meetings, and after she had been "clean" for nine months, she was told about O'Hern House. Today, she is a resident and president of the tenants' association there. She works with the Atlanta CIT, is a contributing member of the community, and is happily reunited with all her family.

There are examples of excellent community-based programs all around the country. We know what to do to help those with serious mental illnesses manage their own conditions and live successfully in their own communities. There are adequate financial resources available to do so, if we simply invest in the right kinds of programs—the ones that we know work—rather than squandering millions and millions of dollars and lives in jails and prisons.

Protecting Our Children: The Most Important Priority of All

During the Christmas holidays several years ago, when our mental health program was working closely with the juvenile justice system in Georgia, two young people died by suicide while in detention. The man in charge of the program was deeply shaken. He remarked about the terrible situation and the effect incarceration has on children—especially those with mental illnesses. "They lose all hope," he said. "Have you ever thought about how long a year is for a twelve-year-old?"

How many other times has this happened, not only in my state, but also in many others?

Each year, more than one and a half million youths enter the juvenile justice system.[25] It is estimated that between two-thirds and three-quarters of them have mental or emotional problems, and of these, 15 percent suffer from a major mental illness.[26]

These statistics are shocking, but even more devastating are the results of a study analyzing whether children in custody received any kind of mental health care. In Chicago, more than 1,800 boys and girls held in the Cook County Juvenile Temporary Detention Center were surveyed. Only about 15 percent of the children with mental disorders got treatment in the detention center, and only about 8 percent received treatment in the community. The number of children who need care and actually receive it is appallingly low.[27]

Carl Bell, MD, has had a tremendous impact on mental health services in Illinois as founder and CEO of Chicago's Community Mental Health Council. He told us that the chief judge for the juvenile detention center in Chicago did not realize until he sat in on a mental health conference how serious the situation had become. According to Carl, the judge "then wrote an order for the county detention center to put a mental health infrastructure in place. Two years later, they had suicide prevention protocols in the detention center." Illinois also began screening all the children in the detention center who got into trouble. "Now kids are being referred to services and sometimes actually being extricated from the criminal justice system for services."[28] This is a much-needed step forward, but what about children with mental illnesses who are incarcerated in other cities around the country?

Sadly, most of the reforms that have occurred in the past few years—including the ones that I have just described—come from the criminal justice system, not from the mental health system. While these reforms are important, they do not address the root causes of the problem. So we continue to waste millions and millions of dollars and tolerate unimaginable suffering and even premature death.

People like Claire, Sophie, David, and Tyler are among a fortunate few whom the criminal justice system has been able to help. But for far too many, like Willie Luke Thurman Jr., help still is not available—and the consequences are deadly. His untimely death was not just a failure of the criminal justice system. He should never have been arrested in the first place.

In the last thirty years we have learned much about the effective use of medications. We have developed small pilot programs, such as Project Interconnections, that offer support and assistance so people can live independently and with dignity in the community. We have seen the creation of peer-to-peer treatment programs that enable people to successfully move toward recovery. Yet millions still have no access at all to these programs. It is not enough to simply bring reforms to the criminal justice system. To help people like Willie, we must embrace comprehensive reform for the entire mental health system. So many lives are at stake.

7.

NEW RESEARCH:
GIVING US REASON
TO HOPE

RESEARCH TRULY PROVIDES THE foundation for progress in the mental health field; it is impossible today to count the lives changed and saved because of new knowledge. When I wrote my last book, *Helping Someone with Mental Illness*,[1] in 1998, we were nearing the end of the Decade of the Brain, a national effort to deepen our understanding of how the brain works. Like many, I was full of hope and optimism about the progress being made in diagnosing and treating mental illnesses. We had learned so much about the biology of these illnesses.[2] In depression, for instance, an imbalance in neurotransmitters in the brain is linked to the problem much the same way that an abnormal level of insulin occurs with diabetes. It was hoped that with proper treatment, the imbalance could be corrected, and often it is. For many, the new knowledge of the role of biology translated into tangible progress in alleviating symptoms and overcoming illnesses.

The National Institute of Mental Health (NIMH) estimates that approximately 95 percent of what we know about the brain today has been learned in the last twenty years. Every day, scientists are making great strides in understanding how it functions and what happens when problems arise. This is especially gratifying to me because it represents the payoff from an investment in mental health research that began when Jimmy was president.

When I was honorary chair of the President's Commission on Mental Health, I visited the NIMH in order to learn more about our federal research activities. Herbert Pardes, MD, the NIMH's director at that time, briefed me about the state of psychiatric research: There were serious problems with quality and focus. Funding was inadequate and too often short-term. When money ran out, important studies were terminated before results could be determined. I was told that though we were on the threshold of new discoveries about the brain, our scientists were discouraged. It was a grim picture of an endeavor that should have been filled with hope and optimism.

The need was so great that our commission called for a 20 percent increase in the NIMH's research budget for 1979,[3] and I am still very proud that Jimmy's budget for that year increased research funding by more than $30 million.[4] In the final report, the commission called for a renewed national commitment to rebuilding our research capacity over the next ten years. Because of budget restrictions, it was impossible to fully fund all the research recommendations, but we significantly reversed the decline in funding for the NIMH that had begun in 1969. The momentum established during Jimmy's administration was essential to reinvigorating the nation's mental health research enterprise, and I believe it formed the basis of the progress we see today.

Some of the advances have been nothing short of amazing. We have new tools in brain imaging that actually allow researchers to watch the brain at work. This has important implications for developing new and more effective treatments. For example, there is a large area at the front of the brain called the prefrontal cortex. It accounts for almost half of the brain in humans. It is very small or almost nonexistent in animals. It is the part of the brain that allows us to think and reason—to be human. With sophisticated imaging machines, neuroscientists studying depression have been able to identify an area in the prefrontal cortex that is overactive when a person is depressed. They have also been able to observe what happens when a person with clinical depression is treated with antidepressants or psychotherapy: This part of the brain seems to become less active. While this work is still in a very experimental stage, it is an important building block in developing more effective interventions for people with clinical depression. It is just one example of the promising strides that have been made in the last thirty years.

Our increased knowledge of brain function has opened up many new possibilities for better understanding mental illnesses. At the same time, another astonishing advancement has made the task even more complex. The Human Genome Project, completed in 2003, identified more than 20,000 human genes—the building blocks of biological code that make each of us unique. The hope in the 1990s was that new knowledge in genetics would make it easier to identify who was at risk for specific mental illnesses and how to more effectively tailor drug therapies for each individual. The reality today is that genes can only provide clues about who might be susceptible or how to target treatments. Neuroscience and genetics are important, but they are just parts of a much larger puzzle.

So today our research agenda must be much broader. We need to understand more clearly the developmental nature of mental illnesses and fundamentally change the way we think about them. We must do a much better job of getting the results of our research and new treatments into the hands of front-line mental health professionals. Experts estimate that today it takes from fifteen to seventeen years for research-based practices to trickle down to the general public.[5] That is a lifetime for a child with a serious mental disorder. We must also use research findings to ensure that public policies are based on better information. Most important, we have to reach out and include people with mental health problems and their families in all of our research efforts. They have knowledge and expertise that are very different from those of research scientists, and without their input our research efforts will fall short. And, we must look carefully at the links between physical and mental health in order to more fully understand the critical role of wellness in recovery.

Redefining Mental Illness: New Hope for the Future

Much of the research focus over the last twenty years relied heavily on what is often called an "acute medical model." Once we learned that the major mental illnesses were biologically based, we thought it would be possible to find a "magic bullet"—a single pill or drug that could cure the disease in the same way that antibiotics can knock out strep throat. New medications for the treatment of depression were introduced with high hopes that their use would significantly reduce the toll the disease takes on millions each year. The same was true regarding drugs for people with schizophrenia. But a major study funded by the NIMH has shown that this is not the case.[6] Overall, the newer drugs do not seem to be more beneficial than the older ones in the trial, although there were some individual benefits for people who did not respond to treatment previously.[7] Researchers are now beginning to think differently about the most effective ways to treat mental illnesses. I asked Thomas Insel, MD, the current director of the NIMH, what the findings meant to him.

"What makes mental illnesses so interesting is that they all have an early onset," he explained. "They are developmental." The initial signs or symptoms begin in childhood and evolve over a lifetime. Half of all people with a serious mental illness are diagnosed by age fourteen.[8] But there's a ten-year gap between the emergence of important symptoms and some-one seeking treatment for them. This means that during the critical years—typically between the ages of fourteen and twenty-four—these young people are at serious risk for all sorts of problems that will threaten their chances to lead full and productive lives as adults.

So, according to Dr. Insel, it's no longer enough to know what works acutely. "For diabetes and heart disease, you want to know what works over many, many years. The same is true for bipolar disease. You need to know what's going to be effective in the long haul. So you begin to think not so much about the magic bullet, but [about] how we detect these disorders very early and develop interventions that are more pre-emptive than preventive. It is a different way of thinking."[9]

The Promise of Early Intervention and Prevention

The implications for research and treatment are clear and offer much more hope. We need to be able to identify these illnesses long before the behaviors or thoughts they produce bring someone to an emergency room. For too long we have been focusing on the end stage of the disease. At best, as with diseases like cancer or heart disease, we are limited in the amount of relief or healing we can achieve. We must therefore shift our priorities and begin to focus on affecting the earliest stages of mental illnesses in children and adolescents. We can even begin to think about better ways to prevent serious mental illnesses.

A new NIMH initiative, Recovery After an Initial Schizophrenic Episode (RAISE), is a first step. It is now recognized that, unlike those who are chronically ill, young people experiencing their first psychotic episode usually respond well to antipsychotic medications. With treatment, they may recover completely from that first event. The important unanswered question is whether function can be preserved and disability forestalled after the first episode with intensive and sustained medical, psychosocial, and rehabilitative intervention. RAISE is investigating this crucial question.

At the Judge Baker Children's Center in Boston, researchers are addressing treatment and prevention at the same time. There, William Beardslee, MD, a member of my Mental Health Task Force and a friend for many years, has been working with families in which a parent is depressed. Through his research, Bill has identified the risks that exist for children when their mother or father is struggling with depression. Bill's work is so important because it enables mental health professionals to give families the tools they need to help heal the depression in the parent and prevent the child from developing depression as well. His intervention, called Family Talk, is changing lives and offering hope to families every day and is now in use in Scandinavia as well as the United States.[10]

Addressing the Chasm

Since Jimmy first called for a dramatic increase in research funding for the NIMH in the 1979 budget, the federal government has invested billions of dollars in mental health research; other private foundations and philanthropic organizations have invested millions more. Yet despite the magnitude of the commitment, much of our knowledge about effective treatments has failed to reach people in need. Because we know that there is a huge gap between the discovery or development of a useful intervention and its adoption in community-based settings, the biggest mental health research problem we face today is not the advancement of knowledge, but translating that research into practice more quickly.

David Shern, PhD, president and CEO of Mental Health America, told me recently that "the area of implementation is where we have a desperate need for more and better science.

"Our field lacks engineers," he said. "We have researchers who do world-class work in discovering and understanding how processes work. . . . But what we don't have are people to design processes to produce outcomes that we know we can produce in laboratory settings."[11]

This notion stuck with me. Imagine a multimillion-dollar highway project whose planners had studied every consequence of the road, from its effects on the environment to those on the surrounding community. Now imagine the project planners had neglected to fund or hire engineers to actually design the road, to implement the ideas discussed in the real world. Such a scenario would be scandalous.

The truth is that the field of mental health has been suffering from the same kind of disorganization and neglect: Many mental health professionals never get access to the best, state-of-the-art treatments, so patients never realize the benefits. The value of clinical and basic research is wasted because routine care rarely incorporates lessons from the laboratory in a timely manner.

A large part of the problem is money. David is particularly concerned about the discrepancies in how new drug treatments are introduced compared to new kinds of talk therapy. The large pharmaceutical companies have a powerful profit incentive to promote rapid and broad-based adoption of new drugs, so they have assumed the responsibility of educating mental health professionals, patients, and families about the benefits of new drugs. Indeed, some argue that they do their job too well and that their extensive marketing campaigns lead to overuse or misuse of very potent medications.

For many, medications have been an important factor in moving toward recovery, but for many more the recovery process requires more extensive interventions—and here the issue is not too much education or promotion, but too little. At the Judge Baker Children's Center, its president, John Weisz, PhD, is working to solve this problem, and his efforts are changing the lives of both mental health professionals and the children they serve. John directs Child STEPS, a network of experts around the country who are using the latest scientific findings to improve mental health care for children and adolescents. Experts are teaching clinicians in community mental health centers about the most effective therapies developed in research institutions and evaluating how well they work in the real world. The results are exciting.[12]

Raceel Jarudi, one of the clinicians working with this project, has seen firsthand how cognitive-behavioral therapy can help children suffering from serious anxiety. Natalie, a ten-year-old girl living in suburban Boston with her parents and younger sister, couldn't sleep by herself, was afraid to go to school, and often spent much of the day crying. Halloween was too scary for her to enjoy; spiders frightened her to death. Her anxiety was disabling. She had been suffering for quite some time, but no one had been able to help.

Using proven Child STEPS techniques and working closely with Natalie's parents, Raceel was able to help her overcome her fears. When she was asked how her life had changed, Natalie smiled and said happily, "Now I can be like other kids; now I can go to sleepovers." This is implementation science at its best, and just think how much more we could accomplish if we increased our investment in building a cadre of "engineers" to carry out this work.

Numbers Matter

The importance of facts and data and sound analysis has been apparent to me ever since Jimmy and I returned to Plains from the Navy to take over the family peanut business. I took full responsibility for managing the books for the business, and I learned then that facts and figures can tell important stories and are critical tools for influencing others and making good decisions.

Throughout my career as a mental health advocate, I have continued to use data and analysis provided by experts across the country to fight stigma and try to improve mental health care. Ronald Kessler, PhD, a noted psychiatric epidemiologist at

Harvard University, talked with me one day about the gaps in our knowledge about how many people actually suffer from specific mental illnesses and why his research into this topic is so necessary. If we don't know how many people are affected, we have no way to make sure that adequate services are available.[13] It seems like a simple idea, but in fact for many problems, like anxiety, we still do not have good data. As a consequence, many who need help do not get it.

His research becomes even more important when we begin to tackle the issue of allocating scarce resources to provide care and treatment, as well as to support basic research. If we are to use these scarce resources most effectively, we must understand the impact of mental illnesses on individuals and our communities. Ron's studies have clearly demonstrated that we are not making good decisions. If you compare how many days of work are lost each year in the United States when people have serious episodes of depression to the number of days of work lost due to hypertension, you will find that depression is a far more costly problem. Yet we spend much more treating hypertension. This kind of research can change the lives of working men and women across our country. If employers act on these compelling data, we can get help to those who are suffering and bring an end to the needless damage that untreated mental illnesses cause every single day.

Ron and I also talked about how difficult it sometimes is to influence government policies and programs with this kind of research. Over the past thirty years I have made hundreds of speeches before Congress and elsewhere stressing the importance of providing equitable mental health coverage in health insurance policies. I explained that not only does it make for a happier, healthier workplace, but research has also shown that it is cost-effective, leading to less absenteeism and job turnover, greater productivity, and better-quality work. Yet neither the insurance companies nor the policy makers in Washington (or even private businesses) would listen.[14]

Finally the Federal Employee Health Benefits Program, one of the largest in the country, with more than eight million enrollees, was amended to provide equal mental health and substance use coverage to federal employees as of January 2001. I remember how long we then waited to get statistics showing the impact of this change. We rejoiced when the evaluation by Howard Goldman, MD, PhD, and his colleagues documented that health care costs did not increase substantially when federal employees had equal mental health coverage.[15] I believe his research provided the irrefutable evidence that allowed the full parity law to be passed by Congress in October 2008. It helped change national policy and brought mental health closer to a level playing field with other conditions.

Out of the Ivory Tower and into the Community

Benjamin Druss, MD, the Rosalynn Carter Chair in Mental Health at the Rollins School of Public Health at Emory University, represents a new breed of researchers who believe that scientific research must be relevant to the people who will ultimately be using it. They are driven by the notion that the best medicines in the world are useless if people don't take them, can't pay for them, or don't even know they exist because they never see a doctor in the first place. To find out what works best, it is essential to engage those who will receive treatment, those who will deliver it, and those who will pay for it. A new treatment method should make sense to real-world providers like clinicians, managers of community mental health centers, human resource directors, and people who run state mental health agencies. The more researchers there are who partner with these people, the more likely it is that the research results will be relevant and useful. Ben comes close to being an engineer.

For the past ten years he has been working on solutions to increase the life expectancy of individuals with chronic mental illnesses who are being cared for by our public mental health system. Ben is trying to find ways to change the shocking and unacceptable fact that their lives are shortened by a full quarter of a century. In one of his projects, he is evaluating whether having a nurse care manager in a community mental health center helps improve patients' health status; in another, he has adapted a chronic disease management program widely used by people with physical illnesses that uses peer-to-peer support to improve overall health through better diet, exercise, and stress management. The nurse care manager study already shows good outcomes. After twelve months, the risk of cardiovascular disease is reduced and patients also report improvements in their mental well-being.[16]

A fast-emerging field called consumer-based participatory research aims to include consumers in designing new interventions. Essential to developing programs that work, this approach focuses on involving consumers at all stages—from developing research questions, to executing an investigation that fits what they want or need, to using and disseminating the results once they are established. If consumers are involved from the very beginning in identifying key interventions that already exist or designing new ones, they have a stake in and a sense of ownership of the results.

Involving consumers in research has also led to the view that to truly help those with serious mental illnesses move toward recovery, we need parallel interventions: not only treatment, but also wellness promotion. Jean Campbell, PhD, of the department of psychiatry at the University of Missouri School of Medicine, heads a $20 million, multisite study that is examining the effectiveness of peer-run programs as adjuncts to traditional mental health services, and she has found that these peer groups really make a difference in the well-being of people who participate in them.

Jean talks about "coming to voice," the concept of putting structure and consciousness to one's experiences as an individual and collectively. "Coming to voice for mental health consumer research becomes a way for people to be able to ask the questions that are meaningful to them and to be able to understand and interpret the results of those questions within their life experience," she says. A well-being study Jean conducted in 1986 was the first mental health consumer research project ever. "The questions were developed by mental health consumers, the interviews were conducted by mental health consumers, and the interpretation of those results was done by mental health consumers," she said. Jean told me that the consumers were also able to initiate a whole new field of inquiry—evaluating the possible negative outcomes produced by the traditional mental health system. "It was a question the traditional system had never asked, but the consumers were able to identify the effects and bring a new focus to an important issue never researched before."[17]

Mind-Body Medicine and the Path to Recovery and Wellness

Gregory Fricchione, MD, a former director of my mental health program at The Carter Center, directs the division of psychiatry and medicine and the Benson-Henry Institute for Mind Body Medicine, both at Massachusetts General Hospital. Greg is in the vanguard of researchers who appreciate the powerful interdependence of health and mental health. For several years he has been studying the impact of stress on a person's health. When a person is under severe stress, the brain has to work very hard to maintain normal blood pressure, heart rate, and temperature, among other things. If a person experiences multiple, continuous stressors, he starts losing the battle. We know from experiments on monkeys that if you insert intravenous lines and pump them full of stress hormones, they will develop obesity, hypertension, high cholesterol, and type 2 diabetes. Some of these same mechanisms may also be at work in humans. If the stress remains overwhelming or persistent, it will take a toll on a person's health—either physically, mentally, or both. Damage will occur in the parts of the body that may be genetically susceptible to illness. When placed in situations of unremitting stress, a person who is born with a genetic propensity to bipolar disorder, depression, or schizophrenia may in fact develop the disease. The same is true for those who are susceptible to asthma, heart disease, or cancer.[18]

At the Benson-Henry Institute, Greg and his colleagues are developing stress-reduction programs for people with serious mental illnesses. He is partnering with a group of consumers to ensure that these resilience-building activities are relevant and effective. The promise of this effort is that it will provide new tools to people with chronic mental illnesses so they can promote their own well-being. It also offers another possible aid in closing the twenty-five-year gap in mortality rates that Ben Druss has been addressing.

Greg's work also confirms the importance of taking a holistic approach to helping those with serious mental or emotional problems. The key to managing stress is building resiliency. Human beings have the capacity to reduce stress in many different ways—through the relaxation response, meditation, exercise, proper nutrition, good sleep habits, and others. Thinking optimistically, believing in a positive future, and having conscious positive expectations about the future are also important, as are having social support and friends, being altruistic, and having spirituality, a sense of connection to something greater than yourself. That whole litany constitutes human resiliency, and it is our most powerful tool in fighting the negative impact of serious mental illnesses.

New Hope

In the 1990s, almost everything we knew about treatments was based on studying large groups of people, but today scientists are concerned with individuals. We now know, for instance, that we can't approach treatments in a "cookie-cutter" fashion. Some people don't respond well to medication but do to psychotherapy, some don't respond to psychotherapy but do to medication, and some need both. Researchers would love to know who is who before they prescribe twelve weeks of a medication. New knowledge in genetics may foster this kind of personalized care. Studies of certain antidepressants may begin to help clinicians predict who will respond best to a particular drug and who will not.

Advances in brain research continue to offer promise. Most exciting to me is our new knowledge that the brain has plasticity throughout life and that conditions once thought irreversible can indeed be altered. This finding opens a whole new way of thinking about serious mental illnesses and about the hope for recovery. Of course, key factors in recovery include having a permanent home and a satisfying job. During the past thirty years we have made great progress in understanding how to provide meaningful help in these critical areas. Consumers have been key in informing this work, and we now know enough to act far more effectively than we currently do.

At the same time, there is always a continuing need for new knowledge. Scientists around the country are gaining the ability to predict who might be at risk for developing schizophrenia and are hoping that early intervention can prevent the full-blown disorder from developing. Dr. Insel, the director of the NIMH, would like to push for even earlier detection: "Where we want to go is detecting psychosis before the very earliest stages—what's called the prodrome [the last stage before the actual development of psychosis]," he says. "We're not there, but my hope is that in ten years, we will be able to find many of the kids who are at high risk and intervene before they even develop the prodrome."[19] That is my hope, too.

8.

RECOVERY:
THE WAY OF THE FUTURE

CHARLES WILLIS GREW UP in Georgia. His early life was filled with hardship and tragedy. Struggling to cope with feelings of loss, grief, and inadequacy, he turned to drugs and alcohol. Thus began a painful journey that endured for years. He couldn't hold a job and was arrested repeatedly for minor offenses. Things got worse and worse. He was diagnosed with chronic depression and for more than ten years was homeless, living in back alleys, and filled with despair.

Today, Charles is Statewide Peer Wellness Initiative director, a program run by the Georgia Mental Health Consumers Network (GMHCN), and a key ally of my mental health program at The Carter Center. In 2009, he participated in one of our events, speaking to an audience of more than three hundred about how the recovery movement had changed his life. "Eight years ago," he said, "I was here in downtown Atlanta at a homeless shelter area, and all that I owned was in a plastic bag, and I had some cardboard under my arm. I was okay. I got up. I stood in soup lines to get food, and I laid around on the cardboard. And believe it or not, because of my illness, the despair associated with it, I thought that was it.

"On February 4, 2001, I went to an AA meeting. I went there for one reason and one reason only—to get a cup of coffee. But in the process of drinking two cups of coffee, there was a gentleman telling his story in the front of the room. And this story sounded just like mine. He was a person who had the same hopes that I once had, but still had been involved in behaviors that were detrimental to his well-being. But he had found a way to live a better life. I was astonished that there was a person just like me who had flown the cuckoo's nest. And I said, 'If he can do it, I can do it.' This was the beginning of a journey to pursue a life that I didn't think was possible for me."[1]

The Emergence of Recovery

The concept of recovery was not even dreamed possible when I first began working in mental health. There was no mention of it in the final report of our President's Commission on Mental Health. Our focus was on gaps in service and access to care. For me, the emergence of recovery as a goal for people with serious mental illnesses represents the single biggest advancement of the last thirty years. Unfortunately, many people today—from the general public to professionals—still know very little about what it is or what it means.

Charles Willis gave a very moving description during our event at The Carter Center. "Despite my mental illness," he said, "I have a lot of strengths and desires. I want to do things with my life, and I have a lot of hope about what my life can be. Recovery is coming to the point where one is defined by things other than the illness. [It is about] feeling well mentally, physically, and spiritually—going beyond the notion that people with mental disorders are *only* the disorder." Recovery shifts the focus from illness to wellness. It recognizes the central role individuals can and must play in managing their own chronic conditions and achieving lives of purpose and fulfillment.

Hope and Despair

Too many people with mental illnesses have been denied that most important human emotion that Charles described—hope. As a consequence, their illnesses completely dominate their lives. Pat Deegan, PhD, an expert on recovery, is a clinical psychologist who was first diagnosed with schizophrenia as a teenager. One day at a conference for people with diverse disabilities, she met a man who was paraplegic.[2]

> At a young age we had both experienced a catastrophic shattering of our worlds, hopes, and dreams. He had broken his neck and was paralyzed, and I was diagnosed as being schizophrenic. We recalled the impact of those first days following the onset of our disabilities. He was an athlete and dreamed of

145

becoming a professional in the sports world. I was a high school athlete and had applied to college to become a gym teacher. Just days earlier we knew ourselves as young people with exciting futures, and then everything collapsed around us. As teenagers, we were told that we had an incurable malady and that we would be "sick" or "disabled" for the rest of our lives. We were told that if we continued with recommended treatments and therapies, we could learn to "adjust" and "cope" from day to day.

Needless to say, we didn't believe our doctors and social workers. In fact, we adamantly denied and raged against these bleak prophesies for our lives. . . . The weeks passed us by but we did not get better. It became harder and harder to believe we would ever be the same again. What initially had seemed like a fleeting bad dream transformed into a deepening nightmare from which we could not awake. We felt like ships floating on a black sea with no course or bearings. We found ourselves drifting farther and farther away from the young, carefree people we had been. He lay horizontal and in traction while his friends were selected to play ball for prestigious colleges. I stood drugged and stiff in the hallways of a mental hospital while my classmates went off to their first year of college. . . .

Our futures appeared to us to be barren, lifeless places in which no dream could be planted and grow into reality. As for the present, it was a numbing succession of meaningless days and nights in a world in which we had no place, no use, and no reason to be. Boredom and wishfulness became our only refuge.

Our denial gave way to despair and anguish. We both gave up. . . . For months I sat in a chair in my family's living room, smoking cigarettes and waiting until it was 8:00 p.m. so I could go back to bed. At this time even the simplest of tasks were overwhelming. I remember being asked to come into the kitchen to help knead some bread dough. I got up, went into the kitchen, and looked at the dough for what seemed an eternity. Then I walked back to my chair and wept. The task seemed overwhelming to me. Later I learned the reason for this: When one lives without hope (when one has given up), the willingness to "do" is paralyzed as well.

All of us who have experienced catastrophic illness and disability know this experience of anguish and despair. It is living in darkness without hope, without a past or a future. It is self-pity. It is hatred of everything that is good and life giving. It is rage turned inward. It is a wound with no mouth, a wound that is so deep that no cry can emanate from it. Anguish is a death from which there appears to be no resurrection. It is inertia which paralyzes the will to do and to accomplish because there is no hope. It is being truly disabled, not by disease or injury, but by despair.

A Short History of the Recovery Movement

In 1978, at the time that I and members of our President's Commission on Mental Health were touring the country listening, gathering information about problems in the mental health system, a new book was published, *On Our Own: Patient-Controlled Alternatives to the Mental Health System*.[3] Written by the late Judi Chamberlin, a consumer who had experienced problems with the traditional system that were similar to those Charles and Pat had, it championed the direct involvement of consumers in their own treatment and made the case for peer-run alternatives to the traditional medical model. The book was revolutionary when it came out.

Judi shared her own experience and expertise with our commission as a member of our working group on legal and ethical issues. For the first time ever, a presidential commission devoted an entire section of its final recommendations to the legal and human rights of people with mental illnesses. Our recommendations were important in addressing steps that would prevent discrimination, guarantee freedom of choice, and ensure appropriate care. In those early days of the movement, attention was focused on involuntary treatment, abuses in psychiatric hospitals, discrimination, and the absence of community supports. All of these are still critical issues, but the early consumer leaders brought to the table a level of political activism that had never before been seen in the mental health field. These efforts led to a new initiative to give consumers a voice in influencing how state mental health programs spent the federal monies they were allocated. Advisory councils with a majority of consumers and family members were created. Joel Slack participated in some of the early meetings, but he soon realized that to have real influence, consumers needed to be in management positions. He was instrumental in establishing the very first Office of Consumer Relations within the Department of Mental Health in Alabama. As its first director, he also played a key role in advising consumers in other states about setting up these new offices.

Today, consumers like Joel hold policy positions at all levels of government. Others, like Pat Deegan, have assumed leadership roles in the mental health professions and are beginning to reshape how providers think about helping people with major mental illnesses. Although the concept of recovery was unheard of at the time of our commission, in 2003 it was one of the key components of the President's New Freedom Commission on Mental Health, which called for "a future where recovery is possible for all people with a mental illness."[4]

Taking Charge of Your Life:
The Individual's Role in Recovery

During the 1990s, the Decade of the Brain, advances in research led many of us in the mental health field to believe that medicine would eventually find a "cure" for the most serious mental illnesses. At the same time, some who were struggling with these illnesses began to speak out about a quite different reality, seriously questioning the value of the medical approach.

"So much of what we were suffering from was over-looked," Pat Deegan said. "The context of our lives was largely ignored. . . . No one asked for our stories. . . . We were told to take medications that made us slur and shake, that robbed our youthful bodies of energy and made us walk stiff like zombies. . . . They kept telling us these medications were good for us, and yet we could feel the high dose of neuroleptics transforming us into empty vessels. We felt like will-less souls or the walking dead. . . . At such high dosages, neuroleptics radically diminished our personhood and sense of self."[5]

Because of the efforts of people like Pat and Joel and Larry Fricks, there is now a different approach to managing serious mental illnesses—one founded on respect and hope and the principle that consumers can and should be full partners in recovery. I asked Larry to describe some of the major differences between the two approaches. "The historical medical model," he told me, "is based on the belief that patients will never be able to function in society. They suffer from impaired judgment and can't trust their own thinking. They don't understand their own needs, and someone else needs to take care of them." This view has often led to long-term hospitalization and the use of massive doses of medication. As Larry said about his own hospitalization, "There were psychiatrists who truly believed that recovery was not possible, that we would never be moved through and out of the system. . . . I was exposed to doctors whose eternal hopelessness was all they offered."[6]

The recovery model, in contrast, is grounded in hope. It is

centered on the individual and based on the belief that individuals with serious mental illnesses can function well and make positive contributions in their own communities. They can take responsibility for their own recovery and can learn from and teach other consumers. Like those who suffer from other chronic illnesses such as diabetes or heart disease, they can manage their own illnesses. Individuals must define the goals of their recovery. For some this may mean going off medication and living symptom-free. For others, it may mean taking medication to help with symptom management. For still others, it may mean experiencing an improvement in quality of life or regaining a sense of purpose and meaning in life. For all, it means having a sense of hope and connection to community.

Larry's own story makes a powerful case for the reality of recovery and the value of this new approach. In 1984, Larry was hospitalized after experiencing a religious conversion, which led to bizarre behavior driven by what he believed God was telling him to do. His marriage had collapsed, his wife had left him, he was drinking heavily, and his business was failing. Diagnosed with bipolar disorder, over the course of a year he endured repeated hospitalizations and experienced firsthand the very worst elements of the medical model. Recovery remained elusive, and he even tried to end his own life—twice. Yet Larry had strengths that were untapped. After his third hospitalization, he made a new pact with God—he would make a new life with new people and places and things.[7]

He began to repay his debts and started to volunteer at a nursing home. He began taking lithium and writing again, selling his columns to the local newspaper. Then one day, at a community meeting on finding a site for a day program for people with serious mental illnesses, he spontaneously went public with his own illness. Outraged by the stigma he felt in the room, he revealed his own history, saying, "The stigma is unbelievable, and we have to give these people a chance." Shortly thereafter he received a call from the state mental health program director, asking him to attend a statewide meeting to set up a mental health consumer network. Thus began a whole new career for Larry, who is now widely recognized as the founder of peer support services, a new type of program that is spreading across the country.

A New Paradigm

Following that initial planning meeting for a consumer network, Larry agreed to serve as volunteer coordinator and organize the first conference of consumers in Georgia, which was held in 1991. He went on to become the first person hired to lead the Office of Consumer Relations and Recovery in the Georgia Division of Mental Health, and in this position, he led the effort to train a new kind of mental health professional: the certified peer specialist. These individuals are revolutionizing the way in which help is provided. Certified peer specialists are people who have experienced the symptoms of a major mental illness. They are in recovery and have completed an extensive training program that gives them the tools necessary to help others. Charles Willis is a good example. In Georgia alone, there are now about five hundred certified peer specialists. The impact of their work has been so great that policy makers and program managers around the country have embraced the concept. Today, certified peer specialists work in more than twenty states, and their ranks are increasing exponentially.

The success of the peer support program is directly tied to the groundbreaking work Larry did to make peer support a Medicaid billable service. It is impossible to overstate the importance of this development. As Larry told me one day, "America values people who do billable work. Being a Medicaid billable service changes everything. People who are incompetent couldn't bill for Medicaid. . . . It is now well known," he continued, "that a job gives us something to do, a reason to get up, a reason to take medicine, a reason to stay well."

Not only does the peer support program create new employment opportunities that enhance self-esteem, but it also gives certified peer specialists financial independence. Being able to bill Medicaid for their services provides sustainable funding for a new workforce in the mental health field, a workforce that has firsthand knowledge of how to successfully combat the debilitating effects of stigma and negative self-image, two factors that still prevent so many people with serious mental illnesses from achieving satisfying and productive lives. Though certified peer specialists are not trained to treat symptoms or deal with medications, they share their experiences and help consumers tap their own reservoirs of strengths and skills to reconnect with family, friends, and community.

Certified peer specialists go through an eight-day training program and then are tested before receiving certification. They are experts in their own right, but their expertise is different than that of traditional mental health professionals, and their impact is powerful. Peers know what it is like to live through a severe depression or a psychotic event. They recognize early warning signs and are familiar with what has worked in the past. They know how to engage in wellness and are able to share this knowledge with others.

While I am disappointed that Medicaid pays for peer support in less than half of all states, I am encouraged that some peer specialist services can be paid for with other public funds. Expanding this program nationwide must be a top priority for all who are concerned about improving the quality of care for people struggling with the most serious mental disorders. It is indeed the future these people deserve.

Full Participation in Community Life

The life stories of Charles, Joel, Pat, and Larry all share a common theme: Recovery is possible when individuals have the supports they need to take advantage of their strengths. A place to live and a job are essential components. We have known how important these elements are for many, many years, yet hundreds of thousands across our country still lack access to these most basic necessities.

One of the best model programs for helping people who are homeless, penniless, and unable to manage their own illnesses and move toward recovery is located in California. The Mental Health America (MHA) Village[8] was established in 1990 after its organizers examined other good programs in our country and combined the best features of each. Over time the Village has demonstrated that people can and do recover even after many years of chronic and disabling mental illnesses. The culture and attitudes of Village staff are what make this level of progress possible. Martha Long, the recently retired founding director of the program, refers to it as the "get a life" program, where staff do "whatever it takes" to help a person in the recovery process. Furthermore, members are considered colleagues in their own recovery process. Rarely is medication prescribed without consulting the members and offering a variety of options. When the member is treated as a partner in the recovery process, medication adherence is no longer an issue for the vast majority.

The outcomes of the program have exceeded all expectations. One of the members from the early homeless outreach program is now supervising about thirty staff members in an additional MHA program, and several former members are now employed on MHA service teams. Many more live independent and productive lives in their own communities. While there are still some who are disabled by their mental illnesses, they are no longer cycling through hospitals and nursing homes, but living in their own apartments and managing their own lives. Today, the MHA Village is a model for recovery-oriented programs throughout California and the rest of the country.

An emerging innovation is consumer-initiated and managed programs. Here in Georgia we have a Peer Wellness Center. It is publicly funded and is an alternative to traditional mental health programs. It focuses on wellness instead of illness. It also has three private rooms which can be used as an alternative to hospitalization. Many who have taken advantage of this option assert that it keeps them from needing inpatient psychiatric care.

A Home, a Job, a Friend

Having a home is fundamental to the recovery process and the catalyst for achieving so many other aspects of a meaningful life. The story of Jerome Lawrence, a talented artist, illustrates this point in a powerful way. During his senior year at Georgia State University, Jerome was diagnosed with paranoid schizophrenia. For the next ten years he struggled unsuccessfully to manage his illness. He experienced hallucinations and sometimes sat motionless for hours, and he thought these were normal behaviors. At other times he would shake uncontrollably. He received Social Security disability benefits and was miserable. He told me one day, "I had always thought that I would become a rich and famous artist, but when my psychiatrist told me that it was not probable, my heart was broken."[9]

Then his psychiatrist introduced a new medication, and Jerome began to take control. He became a regular visitor at a drop-in center, where he connected with the Georgia Mental

Health Consumer Network (GMHCN). Through the network he found the support he needed to begin his recovery journey. One of the staff helped him enroll in an art class at the Church of the Holy Comforter in Atlanta, where many people encouraged him to express himself as an artist.

But he still needed a place to live. In 2002, Habitat for Humanity selected Jerome as the recipient of the first house in Georgia to be built for a person with a serious mental illness. I shall never forget the day of the groundbreaking, when I went to lay the cornerstone. Volunteers from mental health organizations and churches and even mental health consumers from a nearby hospital all came to help build Jerome's house. It was exciting for me to see so many people willing to reach out and help him with his recovery. Jerome's house is a very special place, for it was built with a studio that enables him to pursue his career as an artist—and to support himself and his wife. It gave him a place to work and a way to make a living, and today Jerome is indeed an accomplished artist. Jimmy and I selected one of his paintings—*Tulips Are People II*—for our holiday card in 2008, and two of his paintings grace the walls of The Carter Center.

Jerome's success as an artist—and the beauty of his artwork—offer hope for recovery to all.

Wellness: The New Frontier in Recovery

Those who have the most serious mental illnesses in our public mental health system suffer disproportionately high rates of cardiovascular disease, diabetes, and metabolic diseases;[10] yet in many cases, we could successfully intervene. Risk factors like obesity, smoking, and substance abuse can be prevented or controlled, and access to good medical care and psychiatric medications can be provided. We know what to do, yet we have failed to act.

Our work in Georgia can serve as a model for the rest of the country. In 2006, at the GMHCN's annual convention, the group was besieged with requests for refrigerators to store diabetes medications. It was an "awakening moment" for the leadership, according to executive director Sherry Jenkins Tucker[11], and caused the network to begin to shift its focus to wellness. Whole health is a new concept that calls on professionals to treat the whole person—body, mind, and spirit—not just the mental illness. The group turned to Larry Fricks to develop a program that reduces preventable risk factors for cardiovascular disease and metabolic problems. Called Peer Support Whole Health, the training is designed to increase participants' belief in their own ability to improve their overall health—and it works. Participants are changing behaviors and adopting healthier lifestyles. In another innovation, the GMHCN has adopted a relaxation response module developed by Larry and Greg Fricchione for their peer support counselors. Changing behaviors to promote wellness is becoming a key component of recovery.

Larry and his colleagues at GMHCN have been able to convince the state Medicaid program to reimburse certified peer specialists for helping other peers choose health goals and develop plans to implement them. Promoting whole health recovery is the key to offsetting premature death and disability. Because the vast majority of people with schizophrenia and bipolar disorder are still served by the public mental health system, it is imperative that state Medicaid programs across the country embrace this new approach.

The Keys to Recovery: Hope, Strength, and Respect

Recovery is not linear. People make progress, but they also experience setbacks from time to time. The first step of the journey is the awareness that positive change—a better future—is possible. So many individuals with mental illnesses are led to believe that their cases are hopeless, that there is no chance for recovery. This attitude has been so destructive, bringing nothing but despair. Consumers in the recovery movement are reversing this.

Indeed, the movement is often said to be strength based, which means that when they are in recovery, individuals focus on building their own talents, resilience, and coping skills. One's inherent worth as a human being is valued and validated. Working out of this more positive frame of mind, people recovering from mental illnesses can take on new life roles. They can be partners, friends, parents, caregivers, employees, artists, activists, and peer counselors. They can "get a life."

All of this progress is based on a simple need—respect. "Respect has been, it is, and it will always be the most important ingredient in all of rehabilitation," Joel Slack told me. "If respect is absent in a therapeutic environment, we're compromising everything we've learned about how to take care of people with mental illnesses."

But Joel doesn't mean only that others should respect people with mental illnesses. "I'm talking about respect between staff and patients, but also [about] how professionals need to respect each other in order to honor and value the patient. Patients need to make an effort to be respectful, to deal with their anger and frustration about being disabled. The message of respect is universal." As the founder of Respect International, Joel has delivered this message in educational programs in more than forty countries.

Joel has recovered. He now has a family, a wife and a young daughter. "I live a very fulfilling life. I have a successful business, a healthy life. I spent most of my life trying to recover and manage myself. At forty-three I finally met somebody and fell in love. I started my family and I feel like I have everything that everyone else has. My wife and daughter have helped transform me, to take me from a life of a psychiatric patient to real personhood."[12]

And it is that impulse toward full personhood that I wish for everyone who has lived and struggled with a mental illness. I am sure that one day soon it will be possible—it is within our reach.

ENDNOTES

Introduction

1   The legislation's full name was the Mental Retardation Facilities and Community Mental Health Centers Construction Act of 1963.

2   US Department of Health and Human Services, *Mental Health: Culture, Race, and Ethnicity*, 2001.

Chapter 1

1   Personal communication, January 23, 1977.

2   Carter Center Mental Health Program, *Stigma and the Mentally Ill. What Is Stigma?* Rosalynn Carter Symposium on Mental Health Policy, Atlanta, GA, November 15, 1985.

3   Carter Center Mental Health Program, *Reducing the Stigma of Mental Illnesses in Georgia*, Twelfth Annual Rosalynn Carter Mental Health Forum, Atlanta, GA, May 18, 2007.

4   Jack K. Martin, Bernice A. Pescosolido, and Steven A. Tuch, "Of Fear and Loathing: The Role of 'Disturbing Behavior,' Labels, and Causal Attributions in Shaping Public Attitudes Toward People with Mental Illness," *Journal of Health and Social Behavior* 41(2000): 208–23.

5   Ronald C. Kessler, Wai Tat Chiu, Olga Demler, and Ellen E. Walters, "Prevalence, Severity, and Comorbidity of 12-Month *DSM-IV* Disorders in the National Comorbidity Survey Replication," *Archives of General Psychiatry* 62(2005): 617–27.

6   Richard M. Cohen, *Strong at the Broken Places: Voices of Illness, a Chorus of Hope* (New York: Harper, 2008).

7   Linda A. Teplin, Gary M. McClelland, Karen M. Abram, and Dana A. Weiner, "Crime Victimization in Adults with Severe Mental Illness: Comparison with the National Crime Victimization Survey," *Archives of General Psychiatry* 62(2005): 911–21.

8   US Department of Health and Human Services, *Mental Health: A Report of the Surgeon General* (Rockville, MD: US Department of Health and Human Services, 1999).

9   Patrick W. Corrigan and Amy C. Watson, "Findings from the
     National Comorbidity Survey on the Frequency of Violent Behavior in
     Individuals with Psychiatric Disorders," *Psychiatry Research*
     136(2005): 153–62.

10   Mental Health America, *American Opinions on Mental Health Issues*
     (Alexandria, VA: National Mental Health Association, 1999).

11   Otto F. Wahl, "News Media Portrayal of Mental Illness: Implications
     for Public Policy," *American Behavioral Scientist* 46(2003):
     1594–1600.

12   Donald L. Diefenbach, "The Portrayal of Mental Illness on Prime-
     Time Television," *Journal of Community Psychology* 25(1998):
     289–302.

13   Otto F. Wahl, Amy Wood, and Renee Richards, "Newspaper Coverage
     of Mental Illness: Is It Changing?" *American Journal of Psychiatric
     Rehabilitation* 6(2002): 9–31.

14   Patrick W. Corrigan, Amy C. Watson, Gabriela Gracia, Natalie Slopen,
     Kenneth Rasinski, and Laura L. Hall, "Newspaper Stories as Measures
     of Structural Stigma," *Psychiatric Services* 56(2005): 551–56.

15   Personal communication, July 2007.

16   Mark S. Gold, *The Good News About Depression: Breakthrough
     Medical Treatments that Can Work for You* (New York: Bantam
     Books, 1995), p. 290.

17   Abigail Trafford, "A Disease Called Depression," *Washington Post,*
     November 21, 1995.

Chapter 2

1   Ronald C. Kessler, Wai Tat Chiu, Olga Demler, and Ellen E. Walters,
     "Prevalence, Severity, and Comorbidity of 12-Month *DSM-IV*
     Disorders in the National Comorbidity Survey Replication," *Archives
     of General Psychiatry* 62(2005): 617–27.

2   Ibid.

3   World Health Organization, *The World Health Report 2001: Mental
     Health: New Understanding, New Hope* (Geneva: World Health
     Organization, 2001).

4   Ibid.

5   Kathleen R. Merikangas, Minnie Ames, Lihong Cui, Paul E. Stang, T.
     Bedirhan Ustun, Michael Von Korff, and Ronald C. Kessler, "The
     Impact of Comorbidity of Mental and Physical Conditions on Role
     Disability in the US Adult Household Population," *Archives of General
     Psychiatry* 94(2007): 1180–88.

6   Ronald C. Kessler, Steven Heeringa, Matthew D. Lakoma, Maria
     Petukhova, Agnes E. Rupp, Michael Schoenbaum, Philip S. Wang, and
     Alan M. Zaslavsky, "Individual and Societal Effects of Mental
     Disorders on Earnings in the United States: Results from the National
     Comorbidity Survey Replication," *American Journal of Psychiatry*
     165(2008): 703–11.

7   Samuel Keith, "Schizophrenia: Public Image, Private Reality. Families
     Coping with Mental Illnesses: Improving Public Understanding"
     (keynote address, Sixth Annual Rosalynn Carter Mental Health
     Symposium, Carter Center, Atlanta, GA, October 18, 1990).

8   Ibid.

9   Personal communication, March 13, 2008.

10   World Health Organization, *The World Health Report 2001*, p. 69.

11   Personal communication, April 16, 2008.

12   Elyn R. Saks, *The Center Cannot Hold: My Journey Through Madness*
     (New York: Hyperion, 2007).

13   Mark Morocco, "He's Willing to Be Her Safety Net," *Los Angeles Times*,
     July 9, 2007. http://8.12.42.31/2007/jul/09/health/he-inpractice9.

14   US Department of Health and Human Services, *Mental Health: A
     Report of the Surgeon General* (Rockville, MD: US Department of
     Health and Human Services, 1999).

15   US Census Bureau, *US Summary: 2000*, July 2002. http://www.census.
     gov/prod/2002pubs/c2kprof00-us.pdf.

16   US Department of Health and Human Services, *Mental Health:
     Culture, Race, and Ethnicity: A Supplement to Mental Health: A
     Report of the Surgeon General* (Rockville, MD: US Department of
     Health and Human Services, 2001).

17   Personal communication, November 5, 2007.

18   Institute of Medicine, Committee on Crossing the Quality Chasm,
     "Adaptation to Mental Health and Addictive Disorders," *Improving
     the Quality of Health Care for Mental and Substance-Use Conditions*
     (Washington, DC: National Academies Press, 2006), p. 30.

19   R. Rosenthal, R. E. Levine, D. L. Carlson, et al., "The Shrinking
     Clerkship: Characteristics and Length of Clerkships in Psychiatry
     Undergraduate Education," *Academic Psychiatry* 29 (2005): 47–51.

20   Personal communication, November 4, 2007.

21   Lorraine Echols, "Mental Health Maze Works Against Patients,"
     Atlanta Journal-Constitution, September 26, 2007.

22   T.L. Mark, K.R. Levit, R.M. Coffey, D.R. McKusick, H.J. Harwood,
     E.C. King, E. Bouchery, J.S. Genuardi, R. Vandivort-Warren, J.A. Buck,
     and K. Ryan, "National Expenditures for Mental Health Services and
     Substance Abuse Treatment, 1993–2003," DHHS Publication No.
     SMA 07-4227, 2007.

23 Personal communication, November 4, 2007.

24 Howard H. Goldman, Richard G. Frank, M. Audrey Burnam, Haiden A. Huskamp, M. Susan Ridgely, Sharon-Lise T. Normand, Alexander S. Young, et al., "Behavioral Health Insurance Parity for Federal Employees," *New England Journal of Medicine* 354(2006): 1378–86.

25 David C. Henderson, "From Psychopharmacology to Ethnopsychopharmacology Back to Psychopharmacology," 160th Annual Meeting of the American Psychiatric Association, San Diego, May 19–24, 2007.

26 John Head, *Standing in the Shadows: Understanding and Overcoming Depression in Black Men* (New York: Broadway Books, 2004), p. 22.

27 Alvin Poussaint, "A Heritage of Indifference: We Must Break Down the Walls of Stigma, the Walls of Silence, the Walls of Neglect," *Reducing Disparities: Ethnic Minorities and Mental Health*, Sixteenth Annual Rosalynn Carter Symposium on Mental Health Policy, Atlanta, GA, November 8, 2000.

28 US Department of Health and Human Services, *Mental Health: Culture, Race, and Ethnicity*, 2001.

29 Centers for Disease Control and Prevention, Web-based Injury Statistics Query and Reporting System (WISQARS), Centers for Disease Control and Prevention, 2007. http://www.cdc.gov/injury/wisqars.

30 Ibid.

31 Yeates Conwell and David Brent, "Suicide and Aging I: Patterns of Psychiatric Diagnosis," *International Psychogeriatrics* 7(1995): 149–64.

32 Personal communication, November 4, 2007.

33 Craig W. Colton and Ronald W. Manderscheid, "Congruencies in Increased Mortality Rates, Years of Potential Life Lost, and Causes of Death among Public Mental Health Clients in Eight States," *Preventing Chronic Disease* 3(2006). http://www.cdc.gov/pcd/issues/2006/apr/05_0180.htm.

34 President's New Freedom Commission on Mental Health, "Executive Summary," *Achieving the Promise: Transforming Mental Health Care in America: Final Report*, DHHS Publication No. SMA-03-3831, 2003.

Chapter 3

1 US Department of Health and Human Services, *Mental Health: A Report of the Surgeon General* (Rockville, MD: US Department of Health and Human Services, 1999).

2 Paul Raeburn, "A Childhood Epidemic We Can No Longer Ignore," *USA Today*, September 16, 2004, p. 11A.

3   US Department of Health and Human Services, *Mental Health: A Report of the Surgeon General*, 1999.

4   R.M. Friedman, J.W. Katz-Levey, R. Manderschied, and D. Sondheimer, "Prevalence of Serious Emotional Disturbance in Children and Adolescents," in *Mental Health, United States: 1996*, eds. R. Manderscheid and M. Sonnenschein, DHHS Publication No. SMA-96-3098, pp. 71–88 (Washington, DC: US Government Printing Office, 1996).

5   Lisbeth Schorr, *Within Our Reach: Breaking the Cycle of Disadvantage* (New York: Doubleday, 1988).

6   US Department of Health and Human Services, *Mental Health: A Report of the Surgeon General*.

7   Steve Forness, "Schools and Identification of Mental Health Needs," *Report of the Surgeon General's Conference on Children's Mental Health: A National Action Agenda*, pp. 21–22 (Washington, DC: Department of Health and Human Services, 2000).

8   Los Angeles Unified School District. Cognitive behavioral intervention for trauma in schools. http://www.tsaforschools.org/index.php?option=com_content&task=view&id=81&Itemid=69

9   US Department of Health and Human Services, Administration for Children and Families, *Trends in Foster Care and Adoption—FY 2002–FY 2007*, September 26, 2008. http://www.acf.hhs.gov/programs/cb/stats_research/afcars/trends.htm.

10   Carter Center Mental Health Program, *Transforming Mental Health for Children and Families in Light of the President's New Freedom Commission*, Twentieth Annual Rosalynn Carter Symposium on Mental Health Policy, Atlanta, GA, November 9–10, 2004, p. 22. http://www.cartercenter.org/documents/2099.pdf.

11   Bella English, "Broken," *Boston Globe*, December 4, 2007. p. E1.

12   Kelly J. Kelleher, "Primary Care and Identification of Mental Health Needs," *Report of the Surgeon General's Conference on Children's Mental Health: A National Action Agenda*. http://www.surgeongeneral.gov/topics/cmh/childreport.html.

13   Margaret J. Briggs-Gowan, Sarah McCue Horwitz, Mary E. Schwab-Stone, John M. Leventhal, and Philip J. Leaf, "Mental Health in Pediatric Settings: Distribution of Disorders and Factors Related to Service Use," *Journal of the American Academy of Child and Adolescent Psychiatry* 39(2000): 841–49.

14   Kelly J. Kelleher, "Primary Care and Identification of Mental Health Needs."

15   Timothy E. Wilens, *Straight Talk About Psychiatric Medications for Kids*, 3rd ed. (New York: Guilford Press, 2009). p. 11.

16 Janet Wozniak, Joseph Biederman, Elizabeth Mundy, Douglas Mennin, and Stephen V. Faraone, "A Pilot Family Study of Childhood-Onset Mania," *Journal of the American Academy of Child and Adolescent Psychiatry* 34 (1995): 1577–83.

17 Personal communication, August 9, 2008.

18 Ronald C. Kessler, Patricia Berglund, Olga Demler, Robert Jin, Kathleen R. Merikangas, and Ellen E. Walters, "Lifetime Prevalence and Age-of-Onset Distributions of *DSM-IV* Disorders in the National Comorbidity Survey Replication," *Archives of General Psychiatry* 62(2005): 593–602.

19 Elaine Walker and Anna M. Bollini, "Pubertal Neurodevelopment and the Emergence of Psychotic Symptoms," *Schizophrenia Research* 54(2002): 17–23.

20 System-of-care communities at the comprehensive community mental heath services program for children and their families. http://systemsofcare.samhsa.gov/news/socmap.aspx

21 Janice L. Cooper, Yumiko Aratani, Jane Knitzer, et al. (2008) *Unclaimed Children Revisited: The Status of Children's Mental Health Policy in the United States.* New York: National Center for Children in Poverty.

22 National Research Council and Institute of Medicine. (2009). *Preventing Mental, Emotional, and Behavioral Disorders Among Young People: Progress and Possibilities.* Committee on the Prevention of Mental Disorders and Substance Abuse Among Children, Youth, and Young Adults: Research Advances and Promising Interventions. Mary Ellen O'Connell, Thomas Boat, and Kenneth E. Warner, eds. Board on Children, Youth, and Families, Division of Behavioral and Social Sciences and Education. Washington, DC: The National Academies Press.

23 Institute on Community Integration, College of Education and Human Development, University of Minnesota, Check and Connect, September 28, 2009. http://ici.umn.edu/checkandconnect.

24 Substance Abuse and Mental Health Services Administration, Center for Mental Health Services, *Promotion and Prevention in Mental Health: Strengthening Parenting and Enhancing Child Resilience*, DHHS Publication No. CMHS-SVP-0175, 2007.

25 Mary Ellen O'Connell, Thomas Boat, and Kenneth E. Warner, *Preventing Mental, Emotional, and Behavioral Disorders Among Young People: Progress and Possibilities* (Washington, DC: National Academies Press, 2009).

26 Julie B. Kaplow, Patrick J. Curran, and Kenneth A. Dodge, "Child, Parent, and Peer Predictors of Early-Onset Substance Use: A Multisite Longitudinal Study," *Journal of Abnormal Child Psychology* 30(2002): 199–216.

27   A. Kathryn Power, "Remarks," Twentieth Annual Rosalynn Carter
      Symposium on Mental Health Policy, Atlanta, GA, November 10,
      2004. http://mentalhealth.samhsa.gov/newsroom/speeches/
      120904a.asp.

28   Adele Simmons, "All Children Are Our Children," *Children and
      Families at Risk: Collaborating with Our Schools,* Tenth Annual
      Rosalynn Carter Symposium on Mental Health Policy, Atlanta, GA,
      November 2–3, 1994, p. 12.

29   Julius Richmond, "The Value Commitment," *Children and Families at
      Risk: Collaborating with Our Schools,* Tenth Annual Rosalynn Carter
      Symposium on Mental Health Policy, Atlanta, GA, November 2–3,
      1994, p. 57.

Chapter 4

1   Jimmy and Rosalynn Carter, *Everything to Gain: Making the Most of
      the Rest of Your Life* (New York: Random House, 1987).

2   This is for white males and females. National Center for Health
      Statistics, *Health, United States, 2008, with Chartbook* (Hyattsville,
      MD: National Center for Health Statistics, 2009), p. 218. http://www.
      cdc.gov/nchs/hus/hus08.pdf.

3   International Longevity Center, *Who Cares? Annual Report 2007,*
      International Longevity Center–USA, 2007.

4   D. Steffens, G. Fisher, K. Langa, G. Potter, et al., "Prevalence of
      Depression among Older Americans: The Aging, Demographics and
      Memory Study," *International Psychogeriatrics* 21 (October 2009):
      879–88.

5   US Department of Health and Human Services, Substance Abuse and
      Mental Health Services Administration, Center for Mental Health
      Services, *Mentally Healthy Aging: A Report on Overcoming Stigma for
      Older Americans,* DHHS Publication No. (SMA) 05-3988, 2005, p. 4.

6   Ronald Glaser and Janice K. Kiecolt-Glaser, "Stress-Induced Immune
      Dysfunction: Implications for Health," *Nature Reviews Immunology*
      5(2005): 243–51.

7   A. Rosengren, S. Hawken, S. Ounpuu, K. Sliwa, M. Zubaid, W.A.
      Almahmeed, K.N. Blackett, C. Sitthi-amorn, H. Sato, S. Yusuf, and
      INTERHEART Investigators, "Association of Psychosocial Risk
      Factors with Risk of Acute Myocardial Infarction in 11119 Cases and
      13648 Controls from 52 Countries (the INTERHEART Study): Case-
      Control Study," *Lancet* 364(2004): 953–62.

8   Arialdi M. Miniño, Melanie Horon, and Betty L. Smith, Deaths:
      Preliminary data for 2004, accessed online at www.cdc.gov, on August
      2, 2006; and National Center for Health Statistics, Health, United
      States, 2005: Table 46.

9   Y. Conwell, P.R. Duberstein, C. Cox, J.H. Herrmann, N.T. Forbes, and
    E.D. Caine, "Relationships of Age and Axis I Diagnoses in Victims of
    Completed Suicide: A Psychological Autopsy Study," *American Journal
    of Psychiatry* 153(1996): 1001–8.

10 DHHS, *Mentally Healthy Aging: A Report on Overcoming Stigma in
    Older Adults* (2005): 3. http://download.ncadi.samhsa.gov/ken/pdf/
    SMA05-3988/aging_stigma.pdf,

11 Robert N. Butler, *Why Survive? Being Old in America* (New York:
    Harper and Row, 1975).

12 Ming Tai-Seale, Thomas McGuire, Christopher Colenda, David Rosen,
    and Mary Ann Cook, "Two-Minute Mental Health Care for Elderly
    Patients: Inside Primary Care Visits," *Journal of the American
    Geriatrics Society* 55(2007): 1903–11.

13 Ibid.

14 Institute of Medicine, *Retooling for an Aging America: Building the
    Health Care Workforce,* April 11, 2008.

15 R.N. Butler, J. Estrine, M. Honig, D. Lifsey, C. Muller, and N. O'Brien,
    *A National Crisis: The Need for Geriatric Faculty Training and
    Development* (New York: International Longevity Center, 2002).

16 Melissa Evans, "Who Will Treat the Elderly?" Dailybreeze.com, July
    26, 2008.

17 DHHS, *Mentally Healthy Aging: A Report on Overcoming Stigma in
    Older Adults* (2005): 6. http://download.ncadi.samhsa.gov/ken/pdf/
    SMA05-3988/aging_stigma.pdf,

18 Patients were seen at eighteen primary care clinics in Washington,
    California, Texas, Indiana, and North Carolina. These clinics included
    HMOs, traditional fee-for-service clinics, an independent provider
    association, an inner-city public health clinic, and a Department of
    Veteran's Affairs clinic.

19 J. Unützer, W. Katon, J.W. Williams Jr., C.M. Callahan, L. Harpole,
    E.M. Hunkeler, M. Hoffing, et al., "Improving Primary Care for
    Depression in Late Life: The Design of a Multicenter Randomized
    Trial," *Medical Care* 39(2001): 785–99; and Wayne J. Katon, Michael
    Schoenbaum, Ming-You Fan, Christopher M. Callahan, John Williams
    Jr., Enid Hunkeler, Linda Harpole, et al., "Cost-Effectiveness of
    Improving Primary Care Treatment of Late-Life Depression," *Archives
    of General Psychiatry* 62(2005): 1313–20.

20 Rosalynn Carter, "Addressing the Caregiving Crisis," *Preventing
    Chronic Disease* 5(2008): A02. http://www.cdc.gov/pcd/issues/2008/
    jan/07_0162.htm.

21 Ibid.

22 www.rosalynncarter.org

23 Nori Graham, James Lindesay, Cornelius Katona, José Manoel Bertolote, Vincent Camus, John R. M. Copeland, Carlos A. Mendonça Lima, et al., "Reducing Stigma and Discrimination Against Older People with Mental Disorders: A Technical Consensus Statement," *International Journal of Geriatric Psychiatry* 18(2003): 670–8.

Chapter 5

1 Ronald C. Kessler, Wai Tat Chiu, Olga Demler, and Ellen E. Walters, "Prevalence, Severity, and Comorbidity of 12-Month *DSM-IV* Disorders in the National Comorbidity Survey Replication," *Archives of General Psychiatry* 62(2005): 617–27.

2 Martha S. Gerrity, Kathryn Corson, and Steven K. Dobscha, "Screening for Posttraumatic Stress Disorder in VA Primary Care Patients with Depression Symptoms," *Journal of General Internal Medicine* 22(2007): 1321–4.

3 Arieh Y. Shalev, "Stress versus Traumatic Stress: From Acute Homeostatic Reactions to Chronic Psychopathology," in *Traumatic Stress*, eds. Bessel A. van der Kolk, Alexander C. McFarlane, and Lars Weisaeth, (New York: Guilford Press, 1996) pp. 77–101.

4 Carl Bell, Speech, *Creation of a Self: Color and Trauma in the Life of a Child*, American Psychoanalytic Association Public Forum, New York, December 19, 1997.

5 Vincent J. Felitti, Robert F. Anda, Dale Nordenberg, David F. Williamson, Alison M. Spitz, Valerie Edwards, Mary P. Koss, and James S. Marks, "Relationship of Childhood Abuse and Household Dysfunction to Many of the Leading Causes of Death in Adults: The Adverse Childhood Experiences (ACE) study," *American Journal of Preventive Medicine* 14(1998): 245–58. Dr. Felitti gave the keynote address at our twenty-third annual mental health symposium. Events considered to be "adverse childhood experiences" fall into nine categories: psychological abuse perpetrated by parents; physical abuse perpetrated by parents; sexual abuse perpetrated by anyone; emotional or physical neglect; alcoholism or drug use in the home; loss of a biological parent before the age of eighteen; depression or mental illness in the home; violent treatment of the mother; and incarceration of a household member.

6 Vincent Felitti, "Keynote Panel: Adverse Childhood Experiences Study," *The Time Is Now: Creating a Public Policy Action Agenda on Preventing Mental Illnesses*, Twenty-Third Annual Rosalynn Carter Symposium on Mental Health Policy, Atlanta, GA, November 7–8, 2007.

7 Ibid.

8   Carter Center Mental Health Program, *Mental Health in the Wake of Hurricane Katrina,* Twenty-Second Annual Rosalynn Carter Symposium on Mental Health Policy, Atlanta, GA, November 8–9, 2006.

9   James Cooper, "Keynote Panel: Hurricane Survivors," *Mental Health in the Wake of Hurricane Katrina,* Twenty-Second Annual Rosalynn Carter Symposium on Mental Health Policy, Atlanta, GA, November 8–9, 2006, pp. 5–7.

10 Jeff Wellborn, "Keynote Panel: Hurricane Survivors," *Mental Health in the Wake of Katrina,* Twenty-Second Annual Rosalynn Carter Symposium on Mental Health Policy, Atlanta, GA, November 8–9, 2006, pp. 7–9.

11 Terri Tanielian and Lisa H. Jaycox, eds., "Summary," in *Invisible Wounds of War: Psychological and Cognitive Injuries, Their Consequences, and Services to Assist Recovery* (Santa Monica, CA: Rand Corporation, 2008). http://www.rand.org/pubs/monographs/2008/RAND_MG720.sum.pdf.

12 Ibid.

13 United States Government Accountability Office, *Post-Traumatic Stress Disorder: DoD Needs to Identify the Factors Its Providers Use to Make Mental Health Evaluation Referrals for Servicemembers,* GAO-06-397, May 2006. http://www.gao.gov/new.items/d06397.pdf.

14 Daniel Zwerdling, "Effort Builds to Help 'Forgotten' Troops with PTSD," NPR.org, December 20, 2007. http://www.npr.org/templates/story/story.php?storyId=17362654.

15 Daniel Zwerdling, "Soldiers Say Army Ignores, Punishes Mental Anguish," NPR.org, December 4, 2006. http://www.npr.org/templates/story/story.php?storyId=6576505.

16 Mental Health Advisory Team (MHAT) V. *Operation Iraqi Freedom 06-08: Iraq; Operation Enduring Freedom 8: Afghanistan,* February 14, 2008. p. 28. http://www.armymedicine.army.mil/reports/mhat/mhat_v/MHAT_V_OIFandOEF-Redacted.pdf.

17 Ibid., p. 91.

18 Suicide Risk Management and Surveillance Office, Army Behavioral Health Technology Office, *Army Suicide Event Report (ASER) Calendar Year 2007* (Tacoma, Washington: US Army, 2007). http://media.mcclatchydc.com/smedia/2008/05/29/19/Army-Suicide.source.prod_affiliate.91.pdf.

19 Tanielian, "Summary," *Invisible Wounds of War.*

20 Aaron Levin, "Deployments Take MH Toll on Soldiers and Providers," *Psychiatric News* 43(2008): 1.

21 Robert S. Pynoos and Kathi Nader, "Psychological First Aid and Treatment Approach to Children Exposed to Community Violence: Research Implications," *Journal of Traumatic Stress* 1(1988): 445–73.

Chapter 6

1   Henry J. Steadman, Fred C. Osher, Pamela Clark Robbins, Brian Case, and Steven Samuels, "Prevalence of Serious Mental Illness Among Jail Inmates," *Psychiatric Services* 60(2009): 761–65; Doris J. James and Lauren E. Glaze, "Mental Health Problems of Prison and Jail Inmates," Bureau of Justice Statistics Special Report, Department of Justice, Office of Justice Programs, NCJ 213600, September 2006.

2   Subcommittee on Health and Scientific Research, Committee on Labor and Human Resources, United States Senate, *Hearing on Reappraisal of Mental Health Policy*, Ninety-Sixth Congress, First Session on the Examination of the Recommendations of the President's Commission on Mental Health, February 7, 1979, p. 13.

3   Richard G. Frank and Sherry A. Glied, *Better but Not Well: Mental Health Policy in the United States since 1950* (Baltimore: Johns Hopkins University Press, 2006).

4   Renee Montagne and Steve Inskeep, "Inside the Nation's Largest Mental Institution," *Morning Edition*, NPR.org, August 13, 2008. http://www.npr.org/templates/transcript/transcript. php?storyId=93581736.

5   Andrew A. Skolnick, "Critics Denounce Staffing Jails and Prisons with Physicians Convicted of Misconduct," *JAMA* 280(1998): 1391–2; Wil S. Hylton, "Sick on the Inside: Correctional HMOs and the Coming Prison Plague," *Harper's Magazine*, August 2003, pp. 43–54; American Civil Liberties Union, "ACLU Sues Major Medical Provider Over Deficient Care in Mississippi Prison," news release, June 22, 2005.

6   Michele Gillen, "The Forgotten Floor," WFOR-TV, Miami, September 18–19, 2006. http://www.michelegillen.com/investigations/ forgottenfloor.htm.

7   Personal communication, November 19, 2008.

8   Alina Perez, Steven Leifman, and Ana Estrada, "Reversing the Criminal-ization of Mental Illness," *Crime and Delinquency* 49(2003): 62–78.

9   Ibid.

10   Personal communication.

11   Karen M. Abram and Linda A. Teplin. Co-occurring disorders among mentally ill jail detainees: Implications for public policy. *American Psychologist* 46 (1991): 1036–45.

12   A. Kathryn Power, "Keynote Address," *Mental Health Transformation in Action: Cross-System Collaboration for Consumers and Stakehold-ers*, Miami, March 16, 2007. http://mentalhealth.samhsa.gov/ newsroom/speeches/051607b.asp.

13   Doris J. James and Lauren E. Glaze. Mental health problems of prison and jail inmates. Bureau of Justice Statistics Special Report NCJ 213600, US Department of Justice (September 2006). http://www.ojp. usdoj.gov/bjs/mhppi.htm.

14 National Alliance to End Homelessness, "First Nationwide Estimate of Homeless Population in a Decade Announced," news release, January 10, 2007.

15 County of Santa Clara Legislative Committee, Agenda Item No. 15, "Mental Health Services Act Ballot Initiative," March 16, 2004; *Hope on the Street,* documentary, Michael Isip, producer (San Francisco: KQED, May 2003).

16 Henry J. Steadman, Suzanne M. Morris, and Deborah L. Dennis, "The Diversion of Mentally Ill Persons from Jails to Community-Based Services: A Profile of Programs," *American Journal of Public Health* 85(1995): 1630–5; Henry J. Steadman and Michelle Naples, "Assessing the Effectiveness of Jail Diversion Programs for People with Serious Mental Illness and Co-Occurring Substance Use Disorders," *Behavioral Sciences and the Law* 23(2005): 163–70.

17 Personal communication, March 24, 2008; Theresa D. McClellan, "I Had to Get Some Results: Sister of Inmate Who Died Works with Program to Aid the Mentally Ill," *Grand Rapids Press,* October 10, 2006, p. B1.

18 Randolph Dupont, Sam Cochran, and Sarah Pillsbury, *Crisis Intervention Team Core Elements* (Memphis: University of Memphis CIT Center, September 2007).

19 Henry J. Steadman, Martha Williams Deane, Randy Borum, and Joseph P. Morrissey, "Comparing Outcomes of Major Models of Police Responses to Mental Health Emergencies," *Psychiatric Services* 51(2000): 645–49.

20 R. Dupont and S. Cochran, "Police Response to Mental Health Emergencies: Barriers to Change," *Journal of the American Academy of Psychiatry and the Law* 28(2000): 338–44.

21 Jose A. Martinez, foreperson, "Final Report of the Miami-Dade County Grand Jury: Spring Term A.D. 2004," January 11, 2005, p. 29.

22 Bazelon Center for Mental Health Law, "Disintegrating Systems: The State of States' Mental Health Systems," December 2001.

23 M. Susan Ridgely, John Engberg, Michael D. Greenberg, Susan Turner, Christine DeMartini, and Jacob W. Dembosky, *Justice, Treatment, and Cost: An Evaluation of the Fiscal Impact of Allegheny County Mental Health Court,* Rand Corporation Technical Report TR-439-CSG, 2007.

24 Coalition for Fairness in Mental Illness Coverage, "Mental Illness Parity: Costs of Parity Coverage of Mental Illness," 1998.

25 Melissa Sickmund, e-mail communication, July 21, 2005, as cited in Linda A. Teplin, Karen M. Abram, Gary M. McClelland, Jason J. Washburn, and Ann K. Pikus, "Detecting Mental Disorder in Juvenile Detainees: Who Receives Services," *American Journal of Public Health* 95(2005): 1773–80.

26 Linda A. Teplin, Karen M. Abram, Gary M. McClelland, Mina K. Dulcan, and Amy A. Mericle, "Psychiatric Disorders in Youth in Juvenile Detention," *Archives of General Psychiatry* 59(2002): 1133–43.

27 Linda A. Teplin, Karen M. Abram, Gary M. McClelland, Jason J. Washburn, and Ann K. Pikus, "Detecting Mental Disorder in Juvenile Detainees: Who Receives Services," *American Journal of Public Health* 95(2005): 1773–80.

28 "General Discussion," *Transforming Mental Health for Children and Families in Light of the President's New Freedom Commission,* Twentieth Annual Rosalynn Carter Symposium on Mental Health Policy, Atlanta, GA, November 9–10, 2004. http://www.cartercenter. org/documents/2099.pdf, p. 54.

Chapter 7

1 Rosalynn Carter with Susan K. Golant, *Helping Someone with Mental Illness: A Compassionate Guide for Family, Friends, and Caregivers* (New York: Times Books, 1998).

2 Colm McDonald, Edward T. Bullmore, Pak C. Sham, Xavier Chitnis, Harvey Wickham, Elvira Bramon, and Robin M. Murray, "Association of Genetic Risks for Schizophrenia and Bipolar Disorder with Specific and Generic Brain Structural Endophenotypes," *Archives of General Psychiatry* 61(2004): 974–84.

3 President's Commission on Mental Health, *Report to the President from the President's Commission on Mental Health Vol. 1,* Stock Number 040-000-00390-8 (Washington, DC: US Government Printing Office, 1978).

4 Thomas E. Bryant, Erik J. Meyers, and Kathryn E. Cade, "The American Way with Mental Illness: An Assessment of Public Policy," prepublication report, Public Committee on Mental Health, September 1982.

5 Institute of Medicine, Committee on Crossing the Quality Chasm, *Improving the Quality of Health Care for Mental and Substance-Use Conditions* (Washington, DC: National Academies Press, 2006).

6 Robert A. Rosenheck, Douglas L. Leslie, Jody Sindelar, Edward A. Miller, Haiqun Lin, T. Scott Stroup, Joseph McEvoy, et al., "Cost-Effectiveness of Second-Generation Antipsychotics and Perphenazine in a Randomized Trial of Treatment for Chronic Schizophrenia," *American Journal of Psychiatry* 163(2006): 2080–9.

7 National Institute of Mental Health, "Clinical Antipsychotic Trials of Intervention Effectiveness Study (CATIE): NIMH Study to Guide Treatment Choices for Schizophrenia," March 26, 2009, http://www. nimh.nih.gov/health/trials/practical/catie/index.shtml.

8   Ronald C. Kessler, Patricia Berglund, Olga Demler, Robert Jin, Kathleen R. Merikangas, and Ellen E. Walters, "Lifetime Prevalence and Age-of-Onset Distributions of *DSM-IV* Disorders in the National Comorbidity Survey Replication," *Archives of General Psychiatry* 62(2005): 593–602.

9   Personal communication, March 3, 2009.

10   William R. Beardslee, *Out of the darkened room: When a parent is depressed; protecting the children and strengthening the family* (Boston: Little, Brown and Company, 2002). Dr. Beardslee is director, Baer Prevention Initiatives at Children's Hospital, Boston; senior research scientist at Judge Baker Children's Center; and Gardner/ Monks Professor of Child Psychiatry at Harvard Medical School.

11   Personal communication, March 4, 2009.

12   For more information, see http://www.childsteps.org.

13   Personal communication, March 27, 2009.

14   Personal communication with Philip Wang, November 5, 2007. "In the case of depression, there has been a host of care trials that use a care manager. The care manager is essentially like a nurse but could even be a master's level educator. They help coordinate the person's care to overcome this kind of fragmentation. They encourage people to start treatment if they need it, and help them remain on treatment. The health plan would use a care manager. The trials that have been done in primary care have been consistently positive. They invariably show [that] people who are given this kind of intervention with a care manager have better clinical outcomes. They also are pretty cost-effective. They're not inordinately expensive, but they haven't been taken up. . . . Employers tend not to have picked this up even though it shows that it works, even though there's considerable evidence. So part of what we were doing was not trying to invent something new, but just show these have positive impacts on work outcomes and actually may have monetary value to a purchaser. Those kinds of outcomes have generally been missing."

15   Howard H. Goldman, Richard G. Frank, M. Audrey Burnam, Haiden A. Huskamp, M. Susan Ridgely, Sharon-Lise T. Normand, Alexander S. Young, et al., "Behavioral Health Insurance Parity for Federal Employees," *New England Journal of Medicine* 354(2006): 1378–86.

16   Personal communication, March 4, 2009.

17   Personal communication, March 9, 2009.

18   Personal communication, April 30, 2009.

19   Personal communication, March 3, 2009.

Chapter 8

1   Charles Willis, speech at "Mental Illnesses: Myths and Realities" meeting, Conversations at The Carter Center, Atlanta, GA, April 16, 2009.

2   Patricia E. Deegan, "Recovery: The Lived Experience of Rehabilitation," *Psychosocial Rehabilitation Journal* 11(1988): 11–9.

3   Judi Chamberlin, *On Our Own: Patient-Controlled Alternatives to the Mental Health System* (New York: Hawthorn Books, 1978).

4   New Freedom Commission on Mental Health, *Achieving the Promise: Transforming Mental Health Care in America. Final Report*, DHHS Publication No. SMA-03-3832, 2003.

5   Patricia E. Deegan, "There's a Person in Here," Sixth Annual Mental Health Services Conference of Australia and New Zealand, Brisbane, Australia, September 16, 1996.

6   Richard M. Cohen, *Strong at the Broken Places: Voices of Illness, a Chorus of Hope* (New York: Harper, 2008), pp. 269–70.

7   Ibid., p. 278.

8   For more information, see http://www.mhavillage.org.

9   Jerome Lawrence, "How to Get What You Want By Changing Your Mind: Finding Life Lessons in Art," 2006.

10 Craig W. Colton and Ronald W. Manderscheid, "Congruencies in Increased Mortality Rates, Years of Potential Life Lost, and Causes of Death Among Public Mental Health Clients in Eight States," *Preventing Chronic Disease* 3(2006): 1–14. http://www.cdc.gov/pcd/issues/2006/apr/05_0180.htm.

11 Personal communication.

12 Personal communication, March 13, 2008.

REFERENCES

Abram, Karen M., and Linda A. Teplin. 1991. Co-occurring disorders among mentally ill jail detainees: Implications for public policy. *American Psychologist* 46: 1036–45.

American Civil Liberties Union. 2005. ACLU sues major medical provider over deficient care in Mississippi prison. News release, June 22.

Anonymous. 2007. Clinton hostage-taker says he wanted to die. *USA Today*, December 5.

———. 2007. High rate of suicides seen in soldiers. *Los Angeles Times*, August 16. p. A13.

———. 2004. Media madness: An interview with Dr. Otto Wahl. *Reintegration Today*, Winter. p. 11.

———. 2007. Panel sees no clear aid for veterans under stress. *New York Times*, October 19. p. A23.

Bachman, Ronald E. 2006. If CEOs only knew. HealthcareVisions.net, n.d. http://www.healthcarevisions.net/f/2006_If_CEOs_Only_Knew_v2_with_TABLE.pdf.

Bazelon Center for Mental Health Law. 2001. Disintegrating systems: The state of states' mental health systems. December.

Bell, Carl. 1998. Creation of a self: Color and trauma in the life of a child. Speech presented at the American Psychoanalytic Association Public Forum, New York.

Belluck, Pam. 2006. Living with love, chaos, and Haley. *New York Times*, October 22.

Briggs-Gowan, Margaret J., Sarah McCue Horwitz, Mary E. Schwab-Stone, John M. Leventhal, and Philip J. Leaf. 2000. Mental health in pediatric settings: Distribution of disorders and factors related to service use. *Journal of the American Academy of Child and Adolescent Psychiatry* 39: 841–9.

Brink, Susan. 2008. Mental health sans clichés. *Los Angeles Times*, November 13.

Bryant, Thomas E., Erik J. Meyers, and Kathryn E. Cade. 1982. *The American way with mental illness: An assessment of public policy.* Prepublication report, Public Committee on Mental Health. September.

Butler, R.N., J. Estrine, M. Honig, D. Lifsey, C. Muller, and N. O'Brien. 2002. *A national crisis: The need for geriatric faculty training and development.* New York: International Longevity Center.

Butler, Robert N. 1975. *Why survive? Being old in America.* New York: Harper and Row.

Carrillo, Ernestina. 2001. Assessment and treatment of the Latino patient. In *The Latino Psychiatric Patient: Assessment and Treatment,* eds. Alberto G. Lopez and Ernestina Carrillo. Washington, DC: American Psychiatric Publishing, pp. 38–57.

Carter Center Mental Health Program. 1985. *Stigma and the mentally ill. What is stigma?* Rosalynn Carter Symposium on Mental Health Policy, Atlanta, Georgia, November 15.

———. 2004. *Transforming mental health for children and families in light of the President's New Freedom Commission.* Twentieth Annual Rosalynn Carter Symposium on Mental Health Policy, Atlanta, Georgia, November 9–10. p. 22. http://www.cartercenter.org/documents/2099.pdf.

———. 2004. General discussion. *Transforming mental health for children and families in light of the President's New Freedom Commission.* Twentieth Annual Rosalynn Carter Symposium on Mental Health Policy, Atlanta, Georgia, November 9–10. p. 54. http://www.cartercenter.org/documents/2099.pdf.

———. 2006. *Mental health in the wake of Hurricane Katrina.* Twenty-Second Annual Rosalynn Carter Symposium on Mental Health Policy, Atlanta, Georgia, November 8–9.

———. 2007. *Reducing the stigma of mental illnesses in Georgia.* Twelfth Annual Rosalynn Carter Georgia Mental Health Forum, Atlanta, Georgia, May 18.

Carter, Jimmy, and Rosalynn Carter. 1987. *Everything to gain: Making the most of the rest of your life.* New York: Random House.

Carter, Rosalynn. 1984. *First Lady from Plains.* New York: Fawcett.

———. 2008. Addressing the caregiving crisis. *Preventing Chronic Disease 5* (1): A02. http://www.cdc.gov/pcd/issues/2008/jan/07_0162.htm.

Carter, Rosalynn, with Susan K. Golant. 1994. *Helping yourself help others: A book for caregivers.* New York: Times Books.

———. 1998. Helping someone with mental illness: A compassionate guide for family, friends, and caregivers. New York: Times Books.

Centers for Disease Control and Prevention. 2007. Web-based Injury Statistics Query and Reporting System (WISQARS). Centers for Disease Control and Prevention, 2007. http://www.cdc.gov/injury/wisqars.

Chamberlin, Judi. 1978. *On our own: Patient-controlled alternatives to the mental health system.* New York: Hawthorn Books.

Children's Defense Fund. 2008. *The state of America's children 2008.* December 23. http://www.childrensdefense.org/child-research-data-publications/data/state-of-americas-children-2008-report.pdf.

Coalition for Fairness in Mental Illness Coverage. 1998. *Mental illness parity: Costs of parity coverage of mental illness.*

Cohen, Richard M. 2008. *Strong at the broken places: Voices of illness, a chorus of hope.* New York: Harper.

Colton, Craig W., and Ronald W. Manderscheid. 2006. Congruencies in increased mortality rates, years of potential life lost, and causes of death among public mental health clients in eight states. *Preventing Chronic Disease* 3 (2). http://www.cdc.gov/pcd/issues/2006/apr/05_0180.htm.

Conwell, Yeates, and David Brent. 1995. Suicide and aging I: Patterns of psychiatric diagnosis. *International Psychogeriatrics* 7: 149–64. http://www.cdc.gov/pcd/issues/2006/apr/05_0180.htm.

Conwell, Y., P.R. Duberstein, C. Cox, J.H. Herrmann, N.T. Forbes, and E.D. Caine. 1996. Relationships of age and axis I diagnoses in victims of completed suicide: A psychological autopsy study. *American Journal of Psychiatry* 153: 1001–8.

Cooper, Anderson. 2006. *Dispatches from the edge: A memoir of war, disasters, and survival.* New York: HarperCollins.

Cooper, James. 2006. Keynote panel: Hurricane survivors. In *Mental health in the wake of Hurricane Katrina.* Twenty-Second Annual Rosalynn Carter Symposium on Mental Health Policy, Atlanta, Georgia, November 8–9. pp. 5–7.

Corrigan, Patrick W. n.d. *Beat the stigma and discrimination! Four lessons for mental health advocates.* Chicago: Chicago Consortium for Stigma Research.

Corrigan, Patrick, Fred E. Markowitz, Amy Watson, D. Rowan, and M.A. Kubiak. 2003. An attribution model of public discrimination towards persons with mental illness. *Journal of Health and Social Behavior* 44: 162–79.

Corrigan, Patrick W., and John R. O'Shaughnessy. 2007. Changing mental illness stigma as it exists in the real world. *Australian Psychologist* 42: 90–97.

Corrigan, Patrick W., and Amy C. Watson. 2005. Findings from the National Comorbidity Survey on the frequency of violent behavior in individuals with psychiatric disorders. *Psychiatry Research* 136: 153–62.

Corrigan, Patrick W., Amy C. Watson, Gabriela Gracia, Natalie Slopen, Kenneth Rasinski, and Laura L. Hall. 2005. Newspaper stories as measures of structural stigma. *Psychiatric Services* 56: 551–56.

County of Santa Clara Legislative Committee. 2004. Agenda item no. 15, Mental Health Services Act ballot initiative. March 16.

Curwen, Thomas. 2001. Psychache. *Los Angeles Times,* June 3. http://articles. latimes.com/2001/jun/03/magazine/tm-5874.

Dalton, Carol Chapell. 1977. Why won't you listen? Personal communication and essay, January 23.

Davis, Karen. 2007. Uninsured in America: Problems and possible solutions. *BMJ* 334: 346–48.

Deegan, Patricia E. 1988. Recovery: The lived experience of rehabilitation. *Psychosocial Rehabilitation Journal* 11: 11–19.

———. 1996. There's a person in here. Sixth Annual Mental Health Services Conference of Australia and New Zealand, Brisbane, Australia, September 16.

Department of Policy and Legal Affairs, National Alliance on Mental Illness. n.d. *A guide to mental illness and the criminal justice system: A systems guide for families and consumers.* Arlington, VA: National Alliance on Mental Illness.

Dickey, B., et al., Medical morbidity, mental illness, and substance abuse disorders. *Psychiatric Services* 53 (July 2002): 861-67.

Diefenbach, Donald L. 1998. The portrayal of mental illness on prime-time television. *Journal of Community Psychology* 25: 289–302.

Dupont, R., and S. Cochran. 2000. Police response to mental health emergencies: Barriers to change. *Journal of the American Academy of Psychiatry and the Law* 28: 338–44.

Dupont, Randolph, Sam Cochran, and Sarah Pillsbury. 2007. *Crisis Intervention Team core elements.* September. Memphis: University of Memphis CIT Center.

Echols, Lorraine. 2007. Mental health maze works against patients. *Atlanta Journal Constitution,* September 26.

English, Bella. 2007. Broken. *Boston Globe,* December 4. p. E1.

Evans, Melissa. 2008. Who will treat the elderly? Dailybreeze.com, July 26.

Felitti, Vincent J., Robert F. Anda, Dale Nordenberg, David F. Williamson, Alison M. Spitz, Valerie Edwards, Mary P. Koss, and James S. Marks. 1998. Relationship of childhood abuse and household dysfunction to many of the leading causes of death in adults: The Adverse Childhood Experiences (ACE) study. *American Journal of Preventive Medicine* 14: 245–58.

Felitti, Vincent. 2007. Keynote panel: Adverse Childhood Experiences study. In *The time is now: Creating a public policy action agenda on preventing mental illnesses.* Twenty-Third Annual Rosalynn Carter Symposium on Mental Health Policy, Atlanta, Georgia, November 7–8.

Forness, Steve. 2000. Schools and identification of mental health needs. In *Report of the surgeon general's conference on children's mental health: A national action agenda.* Washington, DC: US Department of Health and Human Services. pp. 21–2.

Frank, Richard G., and Sherry A. Glied. 2006. *Better but not well: Mental health policy in the United States since 1950.* Baltimore: Johns Hopkins University Press.

Friedman, R.M., J.W. Katz-Levey, R. Manderschied, and D. Sondheimer. 1996. Prevalence of serious emotional disturbance in children and adolescents. In *Mental health, United States: 1996,* eds. R. Manderscheid and M. Sonnenschein. DHHS Publication No. SMA-96-3098. Washington, DC: US Government Printing Office. pp. 71–88.

Gates, John. 1996. Fostering resiliency. In *The case for kids: Community strategies for children and families: Promoting positive outcomes.* February 14–16. Atlanta, GA: Carter Center.

Gellene, Denise. 2007. 1 billion mental health days. *Los Angeles Times,* October 2.

Gerrity, Martha S., Kathryn Corson, and Steven K. Dobscha. 2007. Screening for posttraumatic stress disorder in VA primary care patients with depression symptoms. *Journal of General Internal Medicine* 22: 1321–24.

Gillen, Michele. 2006. The forgotten floor. WFOR-TV, Miami, September 18–19. http://www.michelegillen.com/investigations/forgottenfloor.htm.

Glaser, Ronald, and Janice K. Kiecolt-Glaser. 2005. Stress-induced immune dysfunction: Implications for health. *Nature Reviews Immunology* 5: 243–51.

Gold, Mark S. 1995. *The good news about depression: Breakthrough medical treatments that can work for you.* New York: Bantam Books. p. 290.

Goldberg, Carey. 2009. A talk with Judi Chamberlin: Facing death, a plea for the dignity of psychiatric patients. *Boston Globe,* March 22.

Goldman, Howard H., Richard G. Frank, M. Audrey Burnam, Haiden A. Huskamp, M. Susan Ridgely, Sharon-Lise T. Normand, Alexander S. Young, et al. 2006. Behavioral health insurance parity for federal employees. *New England Journal of Medicine* 354: 1378–86.

Graham, Nori, James Lindesay, Cornelius Katona, José Manoel Bertolote, Vincent Camus, John R. M. Copeland, Carlos A. Mendonça Lima, et al. 2003. Reducing stigma and discrimination against older people with mental disorders: A technical consensus statement. *International Journal of Geriatric Psychiatry* 18: 670–78.

Granello, Darcy Haag, and Pamela S. Pauley. 2000. Television viewing habits and their relationship to tolerance toward people with mental illness. *Journal of Mental Health Counseling* 22: 162–75.

Halfon, Neal. 2000. Preschool and identification of mental health needs. *Report of the surgeon general's conference on children's mental health: A national action agenda.* Washington, DC: US Department of Health and Human Services. pp. 24–5.

Head, John. 2004. *Standing in the shadows: Understanding and overcoming depression in black men.* New York: Broadway Books.

Henderson, David C. 2007. *From psychopharmacology to ethnopsychopharmacology back to psychopharmacology.* 160th Annual Meeting of the American Psychiatric Association, San Diego, May 19–24.

Hennessy-Fiske, Molly. 2008. Bed shortage forces L.A. County mental health staff to rely on police. *Los Angeles Times,* November 21. http://articles. latimes.com/2008/nov/21/local/me-mentalhealth21.

Human Rights Watch. 2003. *Ill-equipped: US prisons and offenders with mental illness.* New York: Human Rights Watch. pp. 19–25.

Hylton, Wil S. 2003. Sick on the inside: Correctional HMOs and the coming prison plague. *Harper's Magazine* August. pp. 43–54.

Hyman, Steven E. 2000. Conference proceedings: Summary statements. *Report of the surgeon general's conference on children's mental health: A national action agenda.* Washington, DC: US Department of Health and Human Services. pp. 16–17.

Institute of Medicine, Committee on Crossing the Quality Chasm. 2006. *Improving the quality of health care for mental and substance-use conditions.* Washington, DC: National Academies Press.

Institute of Medicine. 2008. *Retooling for an aging America: Building the health care workforce.* April 11.

Institute on Community Integration, College of Education and Human Development, University of Minnesota. 2009. Check and connect. September 28. http://ici.umn.edu/checkandconnect.

International Longevity Center. 2007. *Who cares? Annual Report 2007.* International Longevity Center–USA.

Isip, Michael, producer. 2003. *Hope on the street,* documentary. San Francisco: KQED, May.

James, Doris J., and Lauren E. Glaze. 2006. Mental health problems of prison and jail inmates. Bureau of Justice Statistics Special Report NCJ 213600, US Department of Justice. September. http://www.ojp.usdoj.gov/bjs/mhpphi.htm.

Jamison, Kay Redfield. 1995. *An unquiet mind: A memoir of mood and madness.* New York: Knopf.

Jaycox, Lisa H., Lindsey K. Morse, Terri Tanielian, and Bradley D. Stein. 2006. *How schools can help students recover from traumatic experiences: A tool kit for supporting long-term recovery.* Santa Monica, CA: Rand Corporation. http://www.rand.org/pubs/technical-_reports/2006/Rand_TR413.pdf.

Jensen, Peter. 2001. Indicators: Early identification is key. *Youth in crisis: Uniting for action.* Seventeenth Annual Rosalynn Carter Symposium on Mental Health Policy. Atlanta, Georgia, November 7–8. p. 35.

Judd, Alan, and Andy Miller. 2007. Lax security, easy escape, tragic ending. *Atlanta Journal Constitution,* January 15.

———. 2008. Mental patients' safety slighted. *Atlanta Journal Constitution,* June 8.

Kaplow, Julie B., Patrick J. Curran, and Kenneth A. Dodge. 2002. Child, parent, and peer predictors of early-onset substance use: A multisite longitudinal study. *Journal of Abnormal Child Psychology* 30: 199–216.

Katon, Wayne J., Michael Schoenbaum, Ming-You Fan, Christopher M. Callahan, John Williams Jr., Enid Hunkeler, Linda Harpole, et al. 2005. Cost-effectiveness of improving primary care treatment of late-life depression. *Archives of General Psychiatry* 62: 1313–20.

Keith, Samuel. 1990. Schizophrenia: Public image, private reality (keynote address). *Families coping with mental illnesses: Improving public understanding.* Sixth Annual Rosalynn Carter Symposium on Mental Health Policy. Atlanta, Georgia, October 18.

Kelleher, Kelly J. Primary care and identification of mental health needs. *Report of the surgeon general's conference on children's mental health: A national action agenda.* Washington, DC: US Department of Health and Human Services. pp. 20–1.

Kennedy, John F. 1963. *Mental illness and mental retardation: Message from the president of the United States relative to mental illness and mental retardation.* Document No. 58, House of Representatives, 88th Congress, 1st Session, February 5.

Kessler, Ronald C., Patricia Berglund, Olga Demler, Robert Jin, Kathleen R. Merikangas, and Ellen E. Walters. 2005. Lifetime prevalence and age-of-onset distributions of *DSM-IV* disorders in the National Comorbidity Survey Replication. *Archives of General Psychiatry* 62: 593–602.

Kessler, Ronald C., Wai Tat Chiu, Olga Demler, and Ellen E. Walters. 2005. Prevalence, severity, and comorbidity of 12-month *DSM-IV* disorders in the National Comorbidity Survey Replication. *Archives of General Psychiatry* 62: 617–27.

Kessler, Ronald C., Steven Heeringa, Matthew D. Lakoma, Maria Petukhova, Agnes E. Rupp, Michael Schoenbaum, Philip S. Wang, and Alan M. Zaslavsky. 2008. Individual and societal effects of mental disorders on earnings in the United States: Results from the National Comorbidity Survey Replication. *American Journal of Psychiatry* 165: 703–11.

Knitzer, Jane. 2004. Strategic implementation panel. *Transforming mental health for children and families in light of the president's New Freedom Commission.* Twentieth Annual Rosalynn Carter Symposium on Mental Health Policy. Atlanta, Georgia, November 9–10. pp. 41–4.

Kristof, Nicholas D. 2008. The luckiest girl. *New York Times,* July 3.

Krug, Etienne G., Linda L. Dahlberg, James A. Mercy, Anthony B. Zwi, and Rafael Lozano, eds. 2002. *World report on violence and health.* Geneva: World Health Organization.

Kupersanin, Eve. 2002. Poor MH care for children called national crisis. *Psychiatric News* 37 (1): 6.

Levin, Aaron. 2006. MH issues get short shrift by primary care docs. *Psychiatric News* 41 (21): 28.

———. 2008. Deployments take MH toll on soldiers and providers. *Psychiatric News* 43 (7): 1.

Link, Bruce G., and Jo C. Phelan. 2001. Conceptualizing stigma. *Annual Review of Sociology* 27: 363–85.

Mark, T.L., K.R. Levit, R.M. Coffey, D.R. McKusick, H.J. Harwood, E.C. King, E. Bouchery, J.S. Genuardi, R. Vandivort-Warren, J.A. Buck, and K. Ryan. 2007. *National expenditures for mental health services and substance abuse treatment, 1993–2003*. DHHS Publication No. SMA 07-4227.

Martin, Jack K., Bernice A. Pescosolido, and Steven A. Tuch. 2000. Of fear and loathing: The role of "disturbing behavior," labels, and causal attributions in shaping public attitudes toward people with mental illness. *Journal of Health and Social Behavior* 41: 208–23.

Martinez, Jose A., foreperson. 2005. *Final report of the Miami-Dade County grand jury: Spring term A.D. 2004*. January 11. p. 29.

Mauer, Barbara J., and Benjamin G. Druss. 2009. Mind and body reunited: Improving care at the behavioral and primary healthcare interface. *Journal of Behavioral Health Services and Research* DOI: 10.1007/s11414-009-9176-0.

McClellan, Theresa D. 2006. I had to get some results: Sister of inmate who died works with program to aid the mentally ill. *Grand Rapids Press,* October 10. p. B1.

McDonald, Colm, Edward T. Bullmore, Pak C. Sham, Xavier Chitnis, Harvey Wickham, Elvira Bramon, and Robin M. Murray. 2004. Association of genetic risks for schizophrenia and bipolar disorder with specific and generic brain structural endophenotypes. *Archives of General Psychiatry* 61: 974–84.

Mental Health Advisory Team (MHAT) V. 2008. *Operation Iraqi Freedom 06-08: Iraq; Operation Enduring Freedom 8: Afghanistan*. February 14. p. 28. http://www.armymedicine.army.mil/reports/mhat/mhat_v/MHAT_V_OIFandOEF-Redacted.pdf.

Mental Health America. 1999. *American opinions on mental health issues.* Alexandria, VA: National Mental Health Association.

Mental Health Policy Resource Center. 1996. Themes and variations: Mental health and substance abuse policy in the making. *Policy in Perspective,* April.

Merikangas, Kathleen R., Minnie Ames, Lihong Cui, Paul E. Stang, T. Bedirhan Ustun, Michael Von Korff, and Ronald C. Kessler. 2007. The impact of comorbidity of mental and physical conditions on role disability in the US adult household population. *Archives of General Psychiatry* 94: 1180–8.

Metzner, Jeffrey L. 2007. Evolving issues in correctional psychiatry. *Psychiatric Times* 24 (10), September 1.

Miller, Greg. 2005. The tsunami's psychological aftermath. *Science* 309: 1030–33.

———. 2006. The unseen: Mental illness's global toll. *Science* 311: 458–61.

Montagne, Renee, and Steve Inskeep. 2008. Inside the nation's largest mental institution. *Morning Edition*, NPR.org, August 13. http://www.npr.org/templates/transcript/transcript.php?storyId=93581736.

Morocco, Mark. 2007. He's willing to be her safety net. *Los Angeles Times*, July 9, p. 3. http://8.12.42.31/2007/jul/09/health/he-inpractice9.

Mulder, Pamela L., Sylvia Shellenberger, Regina Striegel, Pamela Jumper-Thurman, Caroline E. Danda, Mary Beth Kenkel, Madonna G. Constantine, et al. 2000. *The behavioral health care needs of rural women.* Washington, DC: American Psychological Association. http://www.apa.org/rural/ruralwomen.pdf.

Narrow, W.E. n.d. One-year prevalence of depressive disorders among adults 18 and over in the US National Institute of Mental Health Epidemiologic Catchment Area prospective data, unpublished table.

National Alliance on Mental Illness. n.d. *The criminalization of people with mental illness. Policy position.* http://www.nami.org/Content/ContentGroups/Policy/WhereWeStand/The_Criminalization_of_People_with_Mental_Illness___WHERE_WE_STAND.htm.

National Alliance to End Homelessness. 2007. First nationwide estimate of homeless population in a decade announced. News release, January 10.

National Center for Health Statistics. 2009. *Health, United States, 2008, with chartbook.* Hyattsville, MD: National Center for Health Statistics, p. 218. http://www.cdc.gov/nchs/hus/hus08.pdf.

National Child Traumatic Stress Network. 2009. *The effects of trauma on schools and learning.* November 2. http://www.nctsnet.org/nccts/nav.do?pid=ctr_aud_schl_effects.

National GAINS Center, Center for Mental Health Services, Substance Abuse and Mental Health Services Administration, US Department of Health and Human Services. Prevalence of co-occurring mental illness and substance abuse disorders in jail. Spring 2002; revised Winter 2004. http://www.gainscenter.samhsa.gov.

National Institute of Mental Health. 2009. *The impact of mental illness on society.* NIH Publication No. 01-4586. February 13.

———. 2007. Older adults: Depression and suicide facts. April. http://www.nimh.nih.gov/publicat/elderlydepsuicide.cfm.

———. 2009. Clinical Antipsychotic Trials of Intervention Effectiveness study (CATIE): NIMH study to guide treatment choices for schizophrenia. March 26. http://www.nimh.nih.gov/health/trials/practical/catie/index.shtml.

National Research Council and Institute of Medicine. *Depression in parents, parenting and children: Opportunities to improve identification, treatment, and prevention efforts.* Washington, DC: The National Academies Press, 2009. http://www.nap.edu/catalog.php?record_id=12565.

New Freedom Commission on Mental Health. 2003. *Achieving the promise: Transforming mental health care in America. Final report*. DHHS Publication No. SMA-03-3832. Washington, DC: US Department of Health and Human Services.

O'Connell, Mary Ellen, Thomas Boat, and Kenneth E. Warner. 2009. *Preventing mental, emotional, and behavioral disorders among young people: Progress and possibilities*. Washington, DC: National Academies Press.

Osher, David. 2007. Panel II: Prevention programs for adolescents. *The time is now: Creating a public policy action agenda on preventing mental illnesses*. Twenty-Third Annual Rosalynn Carter Symposium on Mental Health Policy, Atlanta, Georgia, November 7–8. pp. 27–9.

Parks, Joe, Dale Svendsen, Patricia Singer, and Mary Ellen Foti, eds. 2006. *Morbidity and mortality in people with serious mental illness*. Alexandria, VA: National Association of State Mental Health Program Directors.

Pearson, Jane L., and Yeates Conwell. 1995. Suicide in late life: Challenges and opportunities for research. *International Psychogeriatrics* 7: 131–6.

Perez, Alina, Steven Leifman, and Ana Estrada. 2003. Reversing the criminalization of mental illness. *Crime and Delinquency* 49: 62–78.

Pescosolido, Bernice A., Jack K. Martin, Bruce G. Link, Saeko Kikuzawa, Giovani Burgos, Ralph Swindle, and Jo Phelan. 1996. *Americans' views of mental health and illness at century's end: Continuity and change*. Indiana Consortium for Mental Health Services Research, Indiana University and The Joseph P. Mailman School of Public Health, Columbia University.

Poussaint, Alvin. 2000. A heritage of indifference: We must break down the walls of stigma, the walls of silence, the walls of neglect. In *Reducing Disparities: Ethnic Minorities and Mental Health*. Sixteenth Annual Rosalynn Carter Symposium on Mental Health Policy, Atlanta, Georgia, November 8.

Power, A. Kathryn. 2004. Remarks. Twentieth Annual Rosalynn Carter Symposium on Mental Health Policy, Atlanta, Georgia, November 10. http://mentalhealth.samhsa.gov/newsroom/speeches/120904a.asp.

———. 2004. Strategic implementation panel. *Transforming mental health for children and families in light of the president's New Freedom Commission*. Twentieth Annual Rosalynn Carter Symposium on Mental Health Policy. Atlanta, Georgia, November 9–10. p. 48.

———. 2007. Keynote address. *Mental health transformation in action: Cross-system collaboration for consumers and stakeholders*. Miami, Florida, May 16. http://mentalhealth.samhsa.gov/newsroom/speeches/051607b.asp.

President's Commission on Mental Health. 1978. *Report to the president from the President's Commission on Mental Health, vol. 1*. Washington, DC: US Government Printing Office, 040-000-00390-8.

President's New Freedom Commission on Mental Health. 2003. Executive summary. In *Achieving the promise: Transforming mental health care in America: Final report.* DHHS Publication No. SMA-03-3831.

Proctor, Bernadette D., and Joseph Dalaker. 2002. *Poverty in the United States: 2001.* Current Population Reports P60-219. Washington, DC: US Government Printing Office.

Pynoos, Robert S., and Kathi Nader. 1988. Psychological first aid and treatment approach to children exposed to community violence: Research implications. *Journal of Traumatic Stress* 1: 445–73.

Raeburn, Paul. 2004. A childhood epidemic we can no longer ignore. *USA Today,* September 16. p. 11A.

———. 2004. *Acquainted with the Night: A Parent's Quest to Understand Depression and Bipolar Disorder in His Children.* New York: Broadway Books.

Ramsay, Claire. 2007. *Felt needs, desired attributes, and acceptability of a depression prevention program for rural caregivers in Georgia.* Master's thesis, Rollins School of Public Health, Emory University.

Regier, D. A., W. E. Narrow, D. S. Rae, R. W. Manderscheid, B. Z. Locke, and F. K. Goodwin. 1993. The de facto US mental and addictive disorders service system. Epidemiologic catchment area prospective 1-year prevalence rates of disorders and services. *Archives of General Psychiatry* 50 (2): 85–94.

Richmond, Julius. 1994. The value of commitment. *Children and families at risk: Collaborating with our schools.* Tenth Annual Rosalynn Carter Mental Health Symposium. Atlanta, Georgia, November 2–3. pp. 56–7.

Ridgely, M. Susan, John Engberg, Michael D. Greenberg, Susan Turner, Christine DeMartini, and Jacob W. Dembosky. 2007. *Justice, treatment, and cost: An evaluation of the fiscal impact of Allegheny County Mental Health Court.* Rand Corporation Technical Report TR-439-CSG.

Roberts, Michelle. 2005. Study finds foster care may foster lifelong ills. *The Oregonian,* April 7.

Rosengren, A., S. Hawken, S. Ounpuu, K. Sliwa, M. Zubaid, W.A. Almahmeed, K.N. Blackett, C. Sitthi-amorn, H. Sato, S. Yusuf, and INTERHEART Investigators. 2004. Association of psychosocial risk factors with risk of acute myocardial infarction in 11,119 cases and 13,648 controls from 52 countries (the INTERHEART Study): Case-control study. *Lancet* 364: 953–62.

Rosenheck, Robert A., Douglas L. Leslie, Jody Sindelar, Edward A. Miller, Haiqun Lin, T. Scott Stroup, Joseph McEvoy, et al. 2006. Cost-effectiveness of second-generation antipsychotics and perphenazine in a randomized trial of treatment for chronic schizophrenia. *American Journal of Psychiatry* 163: 2080–89.

Rosenthal, R., Levine, R. E., Carlson, D. L., et al., 2005. The shrinking clerkship: Characteristics and length of clerkships in psychiatry undergraduate education. *Academic Psychiatry* 29: 47–51.

Rüsch, Nicolas, Matthias C. Angermeyer, and Patrick W. Corrigan. 2005. Mental illness stigma: Concepts, consequences, and initiatives to reduce stigma. *European Psychiatry* 20 (8): 529–39.

Sabol, William J., and Todd D. Minton. 2008. Jail inmates at midyear 2007. In *Bureau of Justice Statistics Bulletin* Department of Justice, Office of Justice Programs, NCJ 221945. June.

Saks, Elyn R. 2007. *The center cannot hold: My journey through madness.* New York: Hyperion.

Scher, Marion. 2006. Stigma—the mark of shame. *South African Psychiatry Review* 9 (2): 118.

Seligman, Martin E. P. 1998. The epidemic of depression among American youth. *Promoting positive and healthy behaviors in children.* Fourteenth Annual Rosalynn Carter Symposium on Mental Health Policy. Atlanta, Georgia, November 18–19. pp. 37–40.

Shain, R.E., and J. Phillips. The stigma of mental illness: Labeling and stereotyping in the news. In L.Wilkins, ed., *Risky Business: Communicating Issues of Science, Risk and Public Policy.* (Westport, CT: Greenwood Press, 1991).

Shalev, Arieh Y. 1996. Stress versus traumatic stress: From acute homeostatic reactions to chronic psychopathology. In *Traumatic Stress,* eds. Bessel A. van der Kolk, Alexander C. McFarlane, and Lars Weisaeth. New York: Guilford Press, pp. 77–101.

Signorielli, N. 1989. The stigma of mental illness on television. *Journal of Broadcast and Electronic Media* 33: 325–31.

Simmons, Adele. 1994. All children are our children. *Children and families at risk: Collaborating with our schools.* Tenth Annual Rosalynn Carter Symposium on Mental Health Policy. Atlanta, Georgia, November 2–3. p. 12.

Skolnick, Andrew A. 1998. Critics denounce staffing jails and prisons with physicians convicted of misconduct. *JAMA* 280: 1391–92.

Solomon, Howard. A CEO and his son. *Business Week*, May 27, 2002.

Steadman, Henry J., Suzanne M. Morris, and Deborah L. Dennis. 1995. The diversion of mentally ill persons from jails to community-based services: A profile of programs. *American Journal of Public Health* 85: 1630–35.

Steadman, Henry J., Edward P. Mulvey, John Monahan, Pamela Clark Robbins, Paul S. Appelbaum, Thomas Grisso, Loren H. Roth, and Eric Silver. 1998. Violence by people discharged from acute psychiatric inpatient facilities and by others in the same neighborhoods. *Archives of General Psychiatry* 55: 393–401.

Steadman, Henry J., and Michelle Naples. 2005. Assessing the effectiveness of jail diversion programs for people with serious mental illness and co-occurring substance use disorders. *Behavioral Sciences and the Law* 23: 163–70.

Steadman, Henry J., Fred C. Osher, Pamela Clark Robbins, Brian Case, and Steven Samuels. 2009. Prevalence of serious mental illness among jail inmates. *Psychiatric Services* 60: 761–65.

Steadman, Henry J., Martha Williams Deane, Randy Borum, and Joseph P. Morrissey. 2000. Comparing outcomes of major models of police responses to mental health emergencies. *Psychiatric Services* 51: 645–49.

Stout, Patricia A., Jorge Villegas, and Nancy A. Jennings. 2004. Images of mental illness in the media: Identifying gaps in the research. *Schizophrenia Bulletin* 30: 543–61.

Subcommittee on Health and Scientific Research, Committee on Labor and Human Resources, United States Senate. 1979. *Hearing on reappraisal of mental health policy.* Ninety-Sixth Congress, First Session on the Examination of the Recommendations of the President's Commission on Mental Health. February 7. p. 13.

Substance Abuse and Mental Health Services Administration, Center for Mental Health Services. 2007. *Promotion and prevention in mental health: Strengthening parenting and enhancing child resilience.* DHHS Publication No. CMHS-SVP-0175.

Suicide Risk Management and Surveillance Office, Army Behavioral Health Technology Office. 2007. *Army Suicide Event Report (ASER) calendar year 2007.* Tacoma, WA: US Army. http://media.mcclatchydc.com/ smedia/2008/05/29/19/Army-Suicide.source.prod_affiliate.91.pdf.

Tai-Seale, Ming, Thomas McGuire, Christopher Colenda, David Rosen, and Mary Ann Cook. 2007. Two-minute mental health care for elderly patients: Inside primary care visits. *Journal of the American Geriatrics Society* 55: 1903–11.

Tanielian, Terri, and Lisa H. Jaycox, eds. 2008. Summary. *Invisible wounds of war: Psychological and cognitive injuries, their consequences, and services to assist recovery.* Santa Monica, CA: Rand Corporation. http://www.rand.org/ pubs/monographs/2008/RAND_MG720.sum.pdf.

Teplin, Linda A., Karen M. Abram, Gary M. McClelland, Mina K. Dulcan, and Amy A. Mericle. 2002. Psychiatric disorders in youth in juvenile detention. *Archives of General Psychiatry* 59: 1133–43.

Teplin, Linda A., Karen M. Abram, Gary M. McClelland, Jason J. Washburn, and Ann K. Pikus. 2005. Detecting mental disorder in juvenile detainees: Who receives services. *American Journal of Public Health* 95: 1773–80.

Teplin, Linda A., Gary M. McClelland, Karen M. Abram, and Dana A. Weiner. 2005. Crime victimization in adults with severe mental illness: Comparison with the National Crime Victimization Survey. *Archives of General Psychiatry* 62: 911–21.

Trafford, Abigail. 1995. A disease called depression. *Washington Post,* November 21.

Treatment Advocacy Center. 2009. Violent behavior: One of the consequences of failing to treat individuals with severe psychiatric disorders. Briefing Paper, April.

Trudeau, Michelle. 2005. Improving mental health care in teen justice system. NPR.org, December 26.

Unützer, J., W. Katon, J.W. Williams Jr., C.M. Callahan, L. Harpole, E.M. Hunkeler, M. Hoffing, et al. 2001. Improving primary care for depression in late life: The design of a multicenter randomized trial. *Medical Care* 39: 785–99.

Unützer, Jürgen, Donald L. Patrick, Greg Simon, David Grembowski, Edward Walker, Carolyn Rutter, and Wayne Katon. 1997. Depressive symptoms and the cost of health services in HMO patients aged 65 years and older. *Journal of the American Medical Association* 277: 1618–23.

US Census Bureau. 2002. *US summary: 2000*. July. http://www.census.gov/prod/2002pubs/c2kprof00-us.pdf.

US Department of Health and Human Services. 1999. *Mental Health: A Report of the Surgeon General*. Rockville, MD: US Department of Health and Human Services.

———. 2001. *Mental health: Culture, race, and ethnicity: A supplement to Mental Health: A Report of the Surgeon General*. Rockville, MD: US Department of Health and Human Services.

US Department of Health and Human Services, Administration for Children and Families. 2008. *Trends in foster care and adoption—FY 2002–FY 2007*. September 26. http://www.acf.hhs.gov/programs/cb/stats_research/afcars/trends.htm.

US Department of Health and Human Services, Substance Abuse and Mental Health Services Administration, Center for Mental Health Services. 2005. *Mentally healthy aging: A report on overcoming stigma for older Americans*. DHHS Publication No. (SMA) 05-3988. Rockville, MD: Substance Abuse and Mental Health Services Administration.

US Department of Health and Human Services, Substance Abuse and Mental Health Services Administration, Center for Mental Health Services. 2007. *Promotion and prevention in mental health: Strengthening parenting and enhancing child resilience*. DHHS Publication No. CMHS-SVP-0175. Rockville, MD: US Department of Health and Human Services.

US Government Accountability Office. 2006. *Post-traumatic stress disorder: DoD needs to identify the factors its providers use to make mental health evaluation referrals for servicemembers*. GAO-06-397, May. http://www.gao.gov/new.items/d06397.pdf.

US Public Health Service. 2000. *Report of the surgeon general's conference on children's mental health: A national action agenda*. Washington, DC: US Department of Health and Human Services.

Wahl, Otto F. 2003. News media portrayal of mental illness: Implications for public policy. *American Behavioral Scientist* 46: 1594–600.

Wahl, Otto F., and J. Narayan. 2006. Structural discrimination against people with mental illness in Connecticut. Poster presentation, Connecticut Psychological Association Convention, Windsor, CT, October 13.

Wahl, Otto F., Amy Wood, and Renee Richards. 2002. Newspaper coverage of mental illness: Is it changing? *American Journal of Psychiatric Rehabilitation* 6: 9–31.

Walker, Elaine, and Anna M. Bollini. 2002. Pubertal neurodevelopment and the emergence of psychotic symptoms. *Schizophrenia Research* 54: 17–23.

Wang, P.S., G.E. Simon, J. Avorn, F. Azocar, E.J. Ludman, J. McCulloch, M.Z. Petukhova, and R.C. Kessler. 2007. Telephone screening, outreach, and care management for depressed workers and impact on clinical and work productivity outcomes. *JAMA* 298: 1401–11.

Wang, Philip S., Sergio Aguilar-Gaxiola, Jordi Alonso, Matthias C. Angermeyer, Guilherme Borges, Evelyn J. Bromet, Ronny Bruffaerts, Giovanni de Girolamo, Ron de Graaf, Oye Gureje, et al. 2007. Use of mental health services for anxiety, mood, and substance disorders in 17 countries in the WHO world mental health surveys. *Lancet* 370: 841–50.

Waters, Rob. 2006. Children in crisis? Concerns about the growing popularity of the bipolar diagnosis. *Psychotherapy Networker,* January/February.

Wellborn, Jeff. 2006. Keynote panel: Hurricane survivors. In *Mental health in the wake of Hurricane Katrina.* Twenty-Second Annual Rosalynn Carter Symposium on Mental Health Policy, Atlanta, Georgia, November 8–9. pp. 7–9.

Wilens, Timothy E. 2009. *Straight talk about psychiatric medications for kids.* 3rd ed. New York: Guilford Press.

Wilkinson, Francis. 2007. The running mate who wasn't. *New York Times Magazine,* December 30. pp. 14–6.

Willis, Charles. 2009. Speech at Mental Illnesses: Myths and Realities meeting. Conversations at The Carter Center, Atlanta, Georgia, April 16.

World Health Organization. 2004. Annex table 3: Burden of disease in DALYs by cause, sex, and mortality stratum in WHO regions, estimates for 2002. In *The World Health Report 2004: Changing History.* Geneva: World Health Organization. pp. 126–31.

———. 2001. *The world health report: 2001: Mental health: New understanding, new hope.* Geneva: World Health Organization.

Wozniak, Janet, Joseph Biederman, Elizabeth Mundy, Douglas Mennin, and Stephen V. Faraone. 1995. A pilot family study of childhood-onset mania. *Journal of the American Academy of Child and Adolescent Psychiatry* 34: 1577–83.

Zwerdling, Daniel. 2006. Soldiers say army ignores, punishes mental anguish. NPR.org. December 4. http://www.npr.org/templates/story/story. php?storyId=6576505.

———. 2007. Effort builds to help "forgotten" troops with PTSD. NPR.org. December 20. http://www.npr.org/templates/story/story.php?storyId=17362654.

RESOURCES
YOU MAY FIND HELPFUL

Information Clearinghouses

National Mental Health Information Center
Center for Mental Health Services
www.mentalhealth.samhsa.gov
PO Box 2345
Rockville, MD 20847-2345
800-789-2647
866-889-2647 (TDD)

National Clearinghouse for Alcohol and Drug Information
www.ncadi.samhsa.gov
PO Box 2345
Rockville, MD 20847-2345
800-729-6686
800-487-4889 (TDD)

National Mental Health Consumers' Self-Help Clearinghouse
www.mhselfhelp.org
1211 Chestnut Street, Suite 1207
Philadelphia, PA 19107
800-553-4539
215-751-1810

Suicide and Crisis Hotlines and Referrals

American Foundation for Suicide Prevention
www.afsp.org
120 Wall Street, 22nd Floor
New York, NY 10005
888-333-2377
212-363-3500
A nonprofit organization committed to understanding and preventing suicide through research, information dissemination, and advocacy work

National Hopeline Network Crisis Hotline, Kristin Brooks Hope Center
www.hopeline.com
1250 24th Street NW, Suite 300
Washington, DC 20037
800-784-2433
A hotline connecting those who are depressed or suicidal to a certified crisis center

National Suicide Prevention Lifeline
www.suicidepreventionlifeline.org
800-273-8255
Toll-free, 24-hour hotline available to anyone in a suicidal crisis or emotional distress

Eating Disorder Referral and Information Center
www.edreferral.com
Information and resource database dedicated to the prevention and treatment of various types of eating disorders

Substance Abuse Treatment Facility Locator
www.findtreatment.samhsa.gov
800-622-4357
A directory of more than 11,000 addiction treatment facilities for adolescents and adults around the country

Facts for Health
www.factsforhealth.org
7617 Mineral Point Road, Suite 300
Madison, WI 53717
608-827-2470
A comprehensive resource to help people identify, understand, and find treatment for social anxiety disorder, premenstrual dysphoric disorder, and post-traumatic stress disorder

Domestic Violence

The National Domestic Violence Hotline
www.ndvh.org
PO Box 161810
Austin, TX 78716
800-799-7233
800-787-3224 (TTY)
A nonprofit organization providing crisis intervention and referral services to victims of domestic violence, their friends, and their family

Helpguide.Org
www.helpguide.org
A nonprofit resource for those suffering from domestic violence, as well as information on a number of other mental and emotional health issues

National Mental Health Organizations and Agencies

Governmental Agencies

National Institute of Mental Health (NIMH)
www.nimh.nih.gov
6001 Executive Boulevard,
Room 8184, MSC 9663
Bethesda, MD 20892-9663
866-615-6464
866-415-8051 (TTY)
A federal research institute working to transform the understanding and treatment of mental illnesses through basic and clinical research, thereby paving the way for prevention, recovery, and cure

Substance Abuse and Mental Health Services Administration (SAMHSA)
www.samhsa.gov
PO Box 2345
Rockville, MD 20847-2345
877-726-4727
800-487-4889 (TTY)
A federal agency dedicated to helping people with mental or substance abuse disorders recover, including help in finding jobs and homes and building strong personal relationships with their peers and family

ADS Center—Resource Center to Promote Acceptance, Dignity, and Social Inclusion Associated with Mental Health
www.adscenter.org
4350 East West Highway, Suite 1100
Bethesda, MD 20814
800-540-0320
A SAMHSA initiative that works to enhance social acceptance of people with mental health problems by providing information and assistance to counteract prejudice and discrimination and promote social inclusion

Professional Representative Organizations

American Psychiatric Association
www.psych.org
1000 Wilson Boulevard, Suite 1825
Arlington, VA 22209-3901
888-357-7924
A medical specialty society of physicians who work toward treatment for all people with mental disorders and substance-related disorders

American Psychological Association
www.apa.org
750 First Street NE
Washington, DC 20002-4242
800-374-2721
202-336-6123 (TDD/TTY)
Represents psychology in the United States with the goals of advancing the communication and application of psychological knowledge in order to improve lives

National Association of Social Workers
www.socialworkers.org
750 First Street NE, Suite 700
Washington, DC 20002-4241
202-408-8600
A member organization for professional social workers that aims to enhance the professional growth and development of its members, create and maintain professional standards, and advance sound social policies

American Counseling Association
www.counseling.org
5999 Stevenson Avenue
Alexandria, VA 22304
800-347-6647
A nonprofit professional and educational organization dedicated to the growth and enhancement of the counseling profession by providing leadership training, publications, educational opportunities, and advocacy services

American Psychiatric Nurses Association
www.apna.org
1555 Wilson Boulevard, Suite 530
Arlington, VA 22209
866-243-2443
A professional membership organization committed to psychiatric mental health nursing, health and wellness promotion through identification of mental health issues, prevention of mental health problems, and the care and treatment of persons with psychiatric disorders

American Association of Pastoral Counseling
http://aapc.org
9504A Lee Highway
Fairfax, VA 22031-2303
703-385-6967
A professional organization whose members represent a broad spectrum of theological and spiritual traditions and work among a wide variety of health care providers and settings

Advocacy Groups

National Alliance on Mental Illness (NAMI)
www.nami.org
3803 North Fairfax Drive, Suite 100
Arlington, VA 22203
800-950-6264
A grassroots advocacy organization that works to improve the lives of people and families affected by mental illnesses, focusing on awareness, education, and advocacy

Mental Health America
www.nmha.org
2000 North Beauregard Street, 6th Floor
Alexandria, VA 22311
800-969-6642
800-433-5959 (TTY)
An organization that seeks to educate the public, encourage reform, and promote the use of effective local and regional prevention and recovery programs

Campaign for Mental Health Reform
www.mhreform.org
1101 15th Street NW, Suite 1212
Washington, DC 20005
A collaborative effort by eighteen national mental health organizations established to seize opportunities resulting from the work of the President's New Freedom Commission on Mental Health by ensuring that the nation's health care system provides access to high-quality and cost-effective mental health care

National Council for Community Behavioral Healthcare
www.nccbh.org
1701 K Street NW, Suite 400
Washington, DC 20006
202-684-7457
Serves more than six million children and adults with mental illnesses and addiction disorders by providing comprehensive, high-quality care that allows for recovery and inclusion in the community

Resources by Disorder

Anxiety Disorders

Anxiety Disorders Association of America
www.adaa.org
8730 Georgia Avenue, Suite 600
Silver Spring, MD 20910
240-485-1001
A national nonprofit association of professionals dedicated to the prevention and treatment of anxiety disorders

National Anxiety Foundation
www.lexington-on-line.com/naf.html
3135 Custer Drive
Lexington, KY 40517-4001
Provides information on anxiety disorders as well as resources to help people seeking further information and care

Social Phobia/Social Anxiety Association
www.socialphobia.org
2058 East Topeka Drive
Phoenix, AZ 85024
A nonprofit organization that provides comprehensive information on anxiety disorders and resources for social phobia

Agoraphobics Building Independent Lives (ABIL)
www.anxietysupport.org
400 West 32nd Street
Richmond, VA 23225
804-353-3687
A grassroots volunteer organization that provides support for and advocates on behalf of people affected by panic attacks and phobias

Personality Disorders

National Education Alliance for Borderline Personality Disorder
www.borderlinepersonalitydisorder.com
PO Box 974
Rye, NY 10580
An organization dedicated to raising public awareness, educating the public, providing support, and promoting research on borderline personality disorder

Treatment and Research Advancements National Association for Personality Disorder
www.tara4bpd.org
23 Greene Street
New York, NY 10013
888-482-7227
212-966-6514
A nonprofit organization that promotes education, research, and treatment of personality disorders and works to reduce stigma

Panic Disorders

The Anxiety Panic Internet Resource
www.algy.com/anxiety
A self-help Internet resource for people with panic disorder and other anxiety disorders

Answers to Your Questions About Panic Disorder
American Psychological Association
www.apa.org/topics/anxiety/panic-disorder.aspx
750 First Street NE
Washington, DC 20002
800-374-2721
202-336-6123 (TDD/TTY)
Provides information on panic disorder, its symptoms, and available treatments

Obsessive-Compulsive Disorder

International OCD Foundation
www.ocfoundation.org
PO Box 961029
Boston, MA 02196
617-973-5801
Works to raise public awareness about obsessive-compulsive disorder by educating families, teachers, caregivers, and legislators

Obsessive Compulsive Anonymous
www.obsessivecompulsive
anonymous.org
PO Box 215
New Hyde Park, NY 11040
516-739-0662
A fellowship of people who share their experiences and hope in order to help one another recover from obsessive-compulsive disorder

Bipolar Disorder

Depression and Bipolar Support Alliance
www.dbsalliance.org
730 North Franklin Street, Suite 501
Chicago, IL 60654
800-826-3632
The leading patient-directed organization for mood disorders; works to ensure that people with bipolar disorder and depression are treated equitably

Lithium Information Center
Madison Institute of Medicine
www.miminc.org
7617 Mineral Point Road, Suite 300
Madison, WI 53717
608-827-2470
Information on lithium and other treatments for bipolar disorder

Manic Depressives Anonymous
www.manicdepressivesanon.org
141 South Ocean Avenue
Atlantic City, NJ 08401
A fellowship of people who share their experiences and inspire hope in one another to stay well through a series of twelve steps

Depression

International Foundation for Research and Education on Depression
www.ifred.org
PO Box 17598
Baltimore, MD 21297-1598
410-268-0044
An organization dedicated to bringing hope to those who suffer from depression by providing them with support and information and by working to combat stigma

Families for Depression Awareness
www.familyaware.org
395 Totten Pond Road, Suite 404
Waltham, MA 02451
781-890-0220
Helps families recognize and cope with depression and other mood disorders and works to reduce stigma and prevent suicides

Depressed Anonymous
www.depressedanon.com
PO Box 17414
Louisville, KY 40217
502-569-1989
An organization that works to provide therapeutic resources for individuals suffering from depression and to prevent depression through education

Postpartum Support International
www.postpartum.net
PO Box 60931
Santa Barbara, CA 93160
800-944-4773
805-967-7636
An organization that works to increase awareness about postpartum depression among public and professional communities

Schizophrenia

Schizophrenia and Related Disorders Alliance of America
www.sardaa.org
PO Box 941222
Houston, TX 77094-8222
240-423-9432
Organization dedicated to providing support to persons with schizophrenia and related disorders

National Alliance for Research on Schizophrenia and Depression (NARSAD)
www.narsad.org
60 Cutter Mill Road, Suite 404
Great Neck, NY 11021
516-829-0091
Raises money from donors around the world and invests it directly in the most promising research projects in mental health disorders, specifically schizophrenia, depression, bipolar disorder, anxiety disorders such as post-traumatic stress disorder and obsessive-compulsive disorder, and childhood disorders that include autism and attention-deficit/ hyperactivity disorder

Schizophrenia.com
www.schizophrenia.com
A nonprofit Web community that provides information and support for individuals, their families, and other caregivers who are affected by schizophrenia

Schizophrenics Anonymous
www.schizophrenia.com
15920 West Twelve Mile Road
Southfield, MI 48076
810-557-6777
A self-help support and fellowship organization administered by the National Schizophrenia Foundation for people with schizophrenia

National Schizophrenia Foundation
403 Seymour Avenue, Suite 202
Lansing, MI 48933
800-482-9534
Seeks to develop and maintain support groups for people with schizophrenia and their families as well as to educate and inform the public about the disorder

Attention Deficit Disorder and Attention-Deficit/ Hyperactivity Disorder

Attention Deficit Disorder Association
www.add.org
PO Box 7557
Wilmington, DE 19803-9997
800-939-1019
An organization for adults with attention deficit disorder dedicated to providing information, resource referrals, and networking opportunities

Children and Adults with Attention Deficit/Hyperactivity Disorder
www.chadd.org
8181 Professional Place, Suite 150
Landover, MD 20785
800-233-4050
301-306-7070
A nonprofit organization providing support, advocacy, and education on medications and treatment for individuals with attention-deficit/ hyperactivity disorder and parents of children with the illness

Attention Deficit Hyperactivity Disorder Information Library
www.newideas.net
A Web site designed for parents that provides information about symptoms of attention-deficit/hyperactivity disorder, treatment options, and medications and their side effects

Post-Traumatic Stress Disorder and Trauma

National Center for Post-Traumatic Stress Disorder
www.ptsd.va.gov
802-296-6300
A center within the Department of Veterans Affairs dedicated to researching traumatic stress and helping veterans and others understand trauma and post-traumatic stress disorder

National Center for Trauma-Informed Care
http://mentalhealth.samhsa.gov/nctic
66 Canal Center Plaza, Suite 302
Alexandria, VA 22314
866-254-4819
A technical assistance center providing education, outreach, and services for trauma-specific care

Tourette's Syndrome

Tourette's Syndrome Association
www.tsa-usa.org
42-40 Bell Boulevard, Suite 205
Bayside, NY 11361-2820
718-224-2999
A national voluntary nonprofit organization that offers referrals to help people and their families cope with the symptoms that occur with Tourette's syndrome

Eating Disorders

National Association of Anorexia Nervosa and Associated Disorders
www.anad.org
PO Box 640
Naperville, IL 60566
630-577-1333
Help line: 630-577-1330
The oldest eating disorder organization in the nation; does advocacy work and provides support and resources for those who suffer from anorexia nervosa and associated disorders

National Eating Disorders Association
www.nationaleatingdisorders.org
603 Stuart Street, Suite 803
Seattle, WA 98101
206-382-3587
Help line: 800-931-2237
An association dedicated to educating, supporting, and providing resources to those affected by eating disorders and their families

Academy for Eating Disorders
www.aedweb.org
111 Deer Lake Road, Suite 100
Deerfield, IL 60015
847-498-4274
A professional association that works to conduct research, education, treatment, and prevention initiatives in the field

Substance Abuse Disorders

Center for Substance Abuse Treatment
www.csat.samhsa.gov
PO Box 2345
Rockville, MD 20847
800-662-4357
800-487-4889 (TDD)
Promotes community-based substance abuse treatment programs for individuals and families and works to improve and expand these services

Center for Substance Abuse Prevention
http://prevention.samhsa.gov
800-729-6686
A federal program that works with states and local populations to develop an effective prevention system in schools, workplaces, and neighborhoods

National Council on Alcoholism and Drug Dependence
www.ncadd.org
244 East 58th Street, 4th Floor
New York, NY 10022
212-269-7797
Hope line: 800-622-2255 (24-hour referrals)
Volunteer organization providing education and information on substance abuse and advocacy to fight stigma

National Institute on Alcohol Abuse and Alcoholism
www.niaaa.nih.gov
5635 Fishers Lane, MSC 9304
Bethesda, MD 20892-9304
301-443-3860
An organization dedicated to reducing alcohol-related problems through research, collaboration, and education of providers, policy makers, and the public

National Institute on Drug Abuse
www.nida.nih.gov
6001 Executive Boulevard, Room 5213
Bethesda, MD 20892-9561
301-443-1124
A federal agency committed to reducing drug abuse and addiction through research and dissemination of results to improve prevention efforts, policy making, and treatment

Center on Addiction and the Family
Phoenix House
www.coaf.org
50 Jay Street
Brooklyn, NY 11201
718-222-6641
A national nonprofit organization that provides education and professional services to children and works to break the cycle of parental substance abuse and reduce the problems that result from parental addiction

Alcoholics Anonymous
www.aa.org
PO Box 459
New York, NY 10163
212-870-3400
A fellowship of people who share their experiences and hope for overcoming their addictions and aiding others who are recovering from alcoholism

Al-Anon/Alateen
www.al-anon.alateen.org
1600 Corporate Landing Parkway
Virginia Beach, VA 23454-5617
757-563-1600
A fellowship of relatives and friends of alcoholics who share their experiences and belief that alcoholism is a family illness and that changing attitudes can help with recovery

Population-Specific Resources

Children's Mental Health

American Academy of Child and Adolescent Psychiatry
www.aacap.org
3615 Wisconsin Avenue NW
Washington, DC 20016-3007
202-966-7300
A nonprofit organization dedicated to understanding and treating childhood mental illnesses by providing services to children and adolescents and working to reduce stigma

Children's Mental Health: Resource List
Mental Health America
www.nmha.org/go/children
2000 North Beauregard Street, 6th Floor
Alexandria, VA 22311
800-969-6642
800-433-5959 (TTY)
Offers a resource guide and links to a Web site especially for teens and young adults with information on mental health issues (www.mpoweryouth.org/411.htm)

Children and Adolescents with Mental, Emotional, and Behavioral Disorders
National Mental Health Information Center
http://mentalhealth.samhsa.gov/publications/allpubs/CA-0006
PO Box 2345
Rockville, MD 20847
800-789-2647
866-889-2647 (TDD)
An overview of mental illnesses that may occur during childhood and adolescence

National Federation of Families for Children's Mental Health
www.ffcmh.org
9605 Medical Center Drive
Rockville, MD 20850
240-403-1901
An organization representing the families of children with mental health needs; believes families have a primary decision-making role in the care their children receive

National Association for Children's Behavioral Health
www.nacbh.org
1025 Connecticut Avenue NW, Suite 1012
Washington, DC 20036
202-857-9735
An organization that advocates on behalf of children and families dealing with emotional and behavioral disturbances by participating in the formulation of policies and laws

American Association of Children's Residential Centers
www.aacrc-dc.org
11700 West Lake Park Drive
Milwaukee, WI 53224
877-332-2272
An organization dedicated to providing a range of residential treatment options for children with behavioral health disorders; includes a comprehensive list of places parents can turn for help

Child and Adolescent Bipolar Foundation
www.bpkids.org
820 Davis Street, Suite 520
Evanston, IL 60201
847-492-8519
A parent-led nonprofit organization that seeks to raise awareness of bipolar disorder and to improve the lives of families raising children and teens affected by the illness

National Child Traumatic Stress
Network
www.nctsn.org
UCLA
11150 West Olympic Boulevard,
Suite 650
Los Angeles, CA 90064
310-235-2633
Duke University
905 West Main Street, Suite 24-E,
Box 50
Durham, NC 27701
919-682-1552
A network established by Congress
in 2001 that works to improve
quality and access to care for
traumatized children, their families,
and communities

AUTISM

Autism Society
www.autism-society.org
7910 Woodmont Avenue, Suite 300
Bethesda, MD 20814-3067
800-328-8476
301-657-0881
A grassroots organization that
provides information about autism,
promotes awareness of the disease,
and advocates for high-quality
services and treatment

National Autism Association
www.nationalautismassociation.org
1330 West Schatz Lane
Nixa, MO 65714
877-622-2884
An organization that educates and
empowers families affected by autism
and raises public awareness of
environmental factors that may cause
neurological damage

College Students and Mental Health

Active Minds
www.activeminds.org
2647 Connecticut Avenue NW,
Suite 200
Washington, DC 20008
202-332-9595
An organization that utilizes students
to promote mental health awareness
and advocacy on college campuses

Bringing Theory to Practice
Association of American Colleges and
Universities
www.aacu.org/bringing_theory
1818 R Street NW
Washington, DC 20009
202-387-3760
A project that sponsors university-
based initiatives encouraging active
engagement in learning in an effort to
enrich students' cognitive and
emotional development

**Community-Campus Partnerships for
Health**
www.ccph.info
UW Box 354809
Seattle, WA 98195-4809
206-666-3406
A nonprofit organization promoting
health on college campuses by
supporting local communities and
building partnerships

Geriatric Mental Health

National Institute on Aging
www.nia.nih.gov
Building 31, Room 5C27
31 Center Drive, MSC 2292
Bethesda, MD 20892
800-222-4225
A federal institute that seeks to
understand the nature of aging
through research and disseminates
health information for older
populations

Geriatric Mental Health Foundation
American Association for Geriatric
Psychiatry
www.aagpgpa.org
7910 Woodmont Avenue, Suite 1050
Bethesda, MD 20814-3004
301-654-7850
Works to raise awareness of mental
health disorders affecting the elderly,
increase access to high-quality mental
health care, and eliminate the stigma
surrounding mental illnesses

American Geriatrics Society
www.americangeriatrics.org
350 Fifth Avenue, Suite 801
New York, NY 10118
212-308-1414
A nonprofit organization of health
professionals dedicated to improving
the health of older Americans by
implementing programs in patient
care, education, and public policy

ALZHEIMER'S

Alzheimer's Disease Education and
Referral Center
National Institute on Aging
www.nia.nih.gov/alzheimers
PO Box 8250
Silver Spring, MD 20907
800-438-4380
Provides information on the diagnosis
and treatment of Alzheimer's for
health professionals, people with
Alzheimer's disease, and their families

Alzheimer's Association
www.alz.org
225 North Michigan Avenue,
Floor 17
Chicago, IL 60601-7633
800-272-3900
866-403-3073 (TDD)
An organization dedicated to
Alzheimer's care, support, and
research with referral services for
information, consultation, and
emergency assistance

Minority Populations

African Americans

Black Mental Health Alliance for
Education and Consultation
www.blackmentalhealth.com
733 West 40th Street, Suite 10
Baltimore, MD 21211
410-338-2642
An organization that provides a
culturally relevant approach to the
development of mental health
programs, support groups, educational programs, and referral services
for African Americans and other
people of color

National Organization for People of
Color Against Suicide
www.nopcas.org
PO Box 75571
Washington, DC 20013
866-899-5317
A nonprofit organization dedicated to
preventing suicide in minority
communities

Factsheet: African Americans
Mental Health America
www.mentalhealthamerica.net/
go/information/get-info/
african-americans
2000 North Beauregard Street,
6th Floor
Alexandria, VA 22311
800-969-6642
800-433-5959 (TTY)
Describes various mental health
disorders as they relate to African
Americans and provides resources for
finding treatment, support, and
medication information

Hispanic Americans

National Resource Center for Hispanic Mental Health
www.nrchmh.org
3575 Quakerbridge Road, Suite 102
Mercerville, NJ 08619
hacosta@nrchmh.org
An organization dedicated to helping individuals with mental illness overcome stigma and seek culturally competent treatment

Latino Mental Health

American Psychiatric Association
http://healthyminds.org
1000 Wilson Boulevard, Suite 1825
Arlington, VA 22209
888-357-7924
Discusses cultural issues related to mental illness and access to care and provides a wealth of information in Spanish

National Latino Behavioral Health Association
www.nlbha.org
1616 P Street NW, Suite 109
Washington, DC 20036
202-797-6530
An organization dedicated to policy work to make behavioral health services more accessible and responsive to the needs of the growing Latino community

Asian Americans

Asian Community Mental Health Services
www.acmhs.org
310 8th Street, Suite 201
Oakland, CA 94607
510-451-6729
12240 San Pablo Avenue
Richmond, CA 94805
510-970-9750
Provides multicultural and multilingual behavioral health care services for children, adolescents, adults, and their families

National Asian American Pacific Islander Mental Health Association
www.naapimha.org
1215 19th Street, Suite A
Denver, CO 80202
303-298-7910
Advocates on behalf of Asian American Pacific Islander consumers and families and provides information about mental disorders in various languages

National Asian Pacific American Families Against Substance Abuse
www.napafasa.org
340 East 2nd Street, Suite 409
Los Angeles, CA 90012
213-625-5795
1016 23rd Street, Suite 201
Sacramento, CA 95816
916-448-5911
A private, nonprofit organization that provides information and resources on substance abuse issues in Asian American Pacific Islander communities

Native Americans

Circles of Care Initiative
Centers for American Indian and Alaska Native Health
http://aianp.uchsc.edu/coc
Mail Stop F800
Nighthorse Campbell Native Health Building
13055 East 17th Avenue
Aurora, CO 80045
303-724-1414
A program that supports communities developing health service programs for children with serious emotional and behavioral disturbances

American Indian Children's Mental Health Programs
National Indian Child Welfare Association
www.nicwa.org/mental_health
5100 SW Macadam Avenue, Suite 300
Portland, OR 97239
503-222-4044
A cooperative effort to provide technical assistance to tribal recipients of various grant programs relating to mental health issues

American Indian and Alaska Native Suicide Prevention Website
Indian Health Service Division of Behavioral Health
www.ihs.gov/NonMedicalPrograms/nspn
801 Thompson Avenue, Suite 300
Rockville, MD 20852
301-443-1539
Provides Native American communities with culturally relevant information regarding suicide prevention and intervention to help them develop their own prevention programs

LGBT Population

Association of Gay and Lesbian Psychiatrists
www.aglp.org
4514 Chester Avenue
Philadelphia, PA 19143-3707
215-222-2800
A community of psychiatrists that works to educate and promote lesbian, gay, bisexual, and transgender mental health issues and provide services for the LGBT community

Alternatives
www.alternativesinc.com
2526 Hyperion Avenue, #4
Los Angeles, CA 90027
800-342-5429
The nation's only gay-owned and -operated alcohol, drug, and mental health program that provides rehabilitation, mental health, and dual-diagnosis treatment to LGBT adults

Lesbian and Gay Child and Adolescent Psychiatric Association
www.lagcapa.org
Contact the American Academy of Child and Adolescent Psychiatry
202-966-7300
An organization that promotes change within the practice of psychiatry to eliminate discrimination based on sexual orientation and gender; especially dedicated to the mental health needs of youth

Legal Issues and Mental Health

Bazelon Center for Mental Health Law
www.bazelon.org
1101 15th Street NW, Suite 1212
Washington, DC 20005
202-467-5730
A leading law advocacy organization for adults and children with mental disabilities

National Center for Mental Health and Juvenile Justice
www.ncmhjj.com
345 Delaware Avenue
Delmar, NY 12054
866-962-6455
Promotes awareness of mental health needs of youth in the juvenile justice system and works to implement improved policies and programs using the best available knowledge

National GAINS Center
Center for Mental Health Services
www.gainscenter.samhsa.gov
800-311-4246
Provides resource referrals for
effective mental health and substance
abuse services for people with dual-
diagnosis disorders who are in
contact with the justice system

National Center for Youth Law
www.youthlaw.org/health
405 14th Street, 15th Floor
Oakland, CA 94612
510-835-8098
An organization that uses the law to
improve the lives of poor and at-risk
children by eliminating barriers to
appropriate health and mental health
care

**National Association for Rights
Protection and Advocacy**
www.narpa.org
PO Box 40585
Tuscaloosa, AL 35404
205-464-0101
An independent organization
comprised of mental health consumers, advocates, and lawyers dedicated
to advancing the rights of people who
are mentally disabled

Information for Caregivers

Family Caregiver Alliance
National Center on Caregiving
www.caregiver.org
180 Montgomery Street, Suite 1100
San Francisco, CA 94104
800-445-8106
415-434-3388
An organization that provides a
public voice for caregivers through
informational, service referral, and
advocacy programs that support
families caring for chronically ill
relatives

**National Family Caregivers
Association**
www.thefamilycaregiver.org
10400 Connecticut Avenue, Suite 500
Kensington, MD 20895-3944
800-896-3650
301-942-6430
An association that works to educate
and empower Americans who care for
loved ones with debilitating or
chronic illnesses

**Rosalynn Carter Institute for
Caregiving**
www.rosalynncarter.org
800 GSW Drive
Georgia Southwestern State University
Americus, GA 31709-4379
229-928-1234
An institute dedicated to recognizing
and supporting caregivers and
individuals coping with chronic illness
and disability

Prescription Assistance

**Partnership for Prescription
Assistance**
www.pparx.org
888-477-2669
An organization that helps qualifying
Americans receive free or reduced-
cost prescription medications and
aims to increase awareness of patient
assistance programs

Together Rx Access
www.togetherrxaccess.com
PO Box 9426
Wilmington, DE 19809-9944
800-444-4106
A prescription savings program
sponsored by various pharmaceutical
companies for US residents who lack
prescription drug coverage

Recovery Movement

National Empowerment Center
www.power2u.org
599 Canal Street
Lawrence, MA 01840
800-769-3728
978-685-1494
An organization promoting recovery, hope, and empowerment for people who suffer from mental illnesses

Respect International
www.respectinternational.org
PO Box 241194
Montgomery, AL 36124
334-546-7885
A nonprofit organization that advocates on behalf of people with psychiatric disorders for their right to be treated with respect and to have basic needs met

Georgia Mental Health Consumer Network
www.gmhcn.org
246 Sycamore Street, Suite 260
Decatur, GA 30030
800-297-6146
404-687-9487
A network that engages with consumers through peer support services and provides education and self-help tools to promote recovery

UPenn Collaborative on Community Integration
University of Pennsylvania School of Medicine
www.upennrrtc.org
3535 Market Street, 3rd Floor—CMHPSR
Philadelphia, PA 19104
215-746-6713
A rehabilitation and research training center focused on helping those with mental health problems build a life in the community

INDEX